M000222851

2017 NAUTILUS SILVER WINNER

Death & Dying / Grief & Loss

ADVANCED PRAISE

"I wish I had had this book when I was 16 and lost both my mom and my way. People told me I should be strong and I didn't know how. Ms. Kapansky-Wright showed me that it was ok to feel what I feel and grieve however I need to grieve. Her writing is sincere, compassionate, and real. This book will support so many in love and grief."

—Dr. Leslie Cornick, Professor and Dean

"*Lamentations of The Sea* will transform your life and your experience with grief and loss. Dr. Kapansky Wright has provided the world with a deeply touching and transformational gift with this book. It's not just a book but a piece of herself and her life that connects to the heart, your heart, of what the experience of loss and healing really is like. Her vulnerability and compassion speak to the needs that all of us humans share when going through life changing experiences such as grief. This book will be my go-to for clients in need of healing, connection, support and compassion, and it will be the go-to for myself when I need to be reminded that I am not alone in my pain and healing. Thank you BethAnne for sending this Light out into the world when we most need it."

—Dr. Gloria Petruzzelli, Clinical Sports Psychologist,
lifewithnolimitscoaching.com

"BethAnne has given us a soulful, brave, honest, and compelling exploration of the depths of grief, written through the lens of her own losses. A collection of beautifully voiced essays, poems, and reflections elucidate the universal journey of protest, sorrow and struggle, and the transformation of grief into hope, personal growth, and profound acceptance. This book is the consummate grief-travelers' companion for the unchosen tour of places both light and dark, exposed in the loss of a loved one."

—Cynthia Bolivar, Licensed Marriage and Family Therapist

"Since I was already familiar with BethAnne's lovely writing, I fully expected to take away a few gems from *Lamentations of The Sea*. But I could never have imagined the depth of this book's brave and heartfelt message of hope and love. This personal invitation into her private world of grief is absolutely spot-on for anyone sadly familiar with the grieving process. It not only spoke, in an achingly beautiful manner, to the worst loss I've ever experienced (that of losing my beloved mom to cancer); it also surprisingly addressed the grief I am currently feeling, trying to adapt to life in a foreign country. I began highlighting my favorite sections in the book, but quickly realized my entire copy was turning yellow! The amazingly poignant way that BethAnne approaches her own healing and the gift of brighter days that her words offer to others are not to be missed. I am forever changed (for the better)."

—April M. Lee, Holistic Life and Wellness Coach,
essence7wellness.com

"Comfort. Compassion. Love. Time. Healing. These messages of hope are thoughtfully and beautifully woven in the pages of *Lamentations of the Sea*. BethAnne's journey is an inspiration and her words are a heartfelt gift for the grieving. Thank you."

—Amy Smith, Licensed Clinical Social Worker

Lamentations of The Sea

Lamentations
OF
The Sea

*111 passages on grief, love, loss
and letting go*

Dr. BethAnne K.W.

2019
GOLDEN DRAGONFLY PRESS

SECOND PRINT EDITION, February 2019
FIRST PRINT EDITION, January 2017
FIRST EBOOK EDITION, January 2017

Cover illustration by BethAnne K.W.
Copyright © 2018 by BethAnne Kapansky Wright.

All rights reserved. No part of this publication may be reproduced
or transmitted in any form or by any means, electronic or otherwise,
without prior written permission by the copyright owner.

ISBN-13: 978-1-7325772-4-4
ISBN-10: 1-7325772-4-2

Library of Congress Control Number: 2018958895

Printed on acid-free paper supplied by a Forest Stewardship Council-certified
provider. Cream paper is made from 30% post-consumer waste recycled material.

First published in the United States of America
by Golden Dragonfly Press, 2019.

www.goldendragonflypress.com

Dedicated to anyone who has ever loved and lost.

CONTENTS

Spring: Grief's Rebirth

Fall: Grief's Release

Foreword

*I*t's been a few years since I wrote the words in *Lamentations of The Sea*, which tells the story of my initial grief journey when I lost my brother Brent.

In that time, I have realized that the journey of the griever is a sacred journey, and though I believe we can come through grief whole and rearranged, I also know I will forever be grieving the loss of Brent. These days I see my grief for exactly what it is: a testament to love. I feel it is my honor and my joy to feel that grief, as it means I now carry Brent in my heart. Always.

Something else that has happened since I first wrote this book is that *Lamentations* was awarded a 2017 Silver Nautilus Award in the category of Death & Dying/Grief & Loss. I am beyond honored by this, and it is a gift to my heart to know my words are touching others and helping them find healing along their grief journeys.

It was tempting to re-edit the words in this Second Edition, as my writing style has changed since I initially wrote the manuscript. Then I realized that the words in these pages are perfect the way they are. Real, passionate, raw, reflective of my writing style at the time, and utterly brave in their vulnerability.

I've chosen to let my words stand exactly as is. I see that as a way to pay homage to my younger 2016 self, who was incredibly courageous for creating this work in the first place, inviting others into her heart, and journeying through the worst of her grief with such naked, tender transparency.

I hope you can feel the love, the truth, and the hope in them, and I hope they help your heart too.

Love,
BethAnne

With Warmest Welcome

When I first began to write *Lamentations of The Sea*, I wanted the pages to feel like a friend. The kind of friend you would call after a great loss so you could sit down over a hot cup of cocoa and have a good talk. The kind of friend that leaves your heart feeling a little more full. The kind of friend who is just as comfortable with conversation as with silence, with laughter as with tears, with love as with loss.

I have come to believe that we will never find any griefs that are the same. We could ask 100 different people what their experience is with loss and how they made it through, and we would get 100 different answers. There are no two grief passages alike; we all have our unique ways of doing things in this world. But there are universal themes when it comes to loving and losing, and my hope is that the contents of this book capture some of those themes and help somebody feel a little more comforted, a little more understood, and a little more connected in their own process of loss.

I've had various experiences with grief throughout my life: a handful of heart aches and heart breaks, the sadness and life change of divorce, the loss of one incredibly Loved Dog, and many years of working as a Psychologist helping other people process and find healing for their own stories of loss. But it was really in January of 2016 that grief came knocking at my front door and let itself in without invitation, want, or welcome. My brother, only one year older than myself and my only sibling, died on January 18, 2016, from a blood clot that broke off into his blood stream and went to his brain. His death was instantaneous, and my life was instantly changed in that moment.

This book is not a detached clinical exploration of grief. It is an experiential book and a story told as it was being lived. It is an "I know what it's like to bleed. So if you are bleeding too, let me share my heart and bones and blood with you and hope it helps you find strength along the way." The selection of personal essays, prose, poetry and reflections on loss not only address core experiences, feelings and processes surrounding grief, but also tell my story of losing my brother, grappling with my own grief, and finding solace and light on my journey.

While I have organized the following pages in the order of the themes and seasons in which they were written, I want *Lamentations of The Sea* to be something you can read start to finish or just pick up, flip through, and find a passage that resonates and feels friendly on that particular day. I want it to be the kind of book I wish I had back in the Winter of 2016 where the story begins.

Though my original impetus for this book was to reflect on grief, I found as I began writing and assembling its pages that it became much more than that. It's a story of how love heals and redeems us. It's a meditation on how life will always come back around again in new forms. It's a tribute to how we can find something beautiful in something that seems broken. There are hope and restoration in these pages.

Last, I am a shameless, wanton, unabashed Gladiator of Love. I believe in Love's healing power. I believe in Love's ability to bind together what's broken and make it whole. I believe Love comes into our lives in many forms, and we are here to learn about those forms, so we can grow our hearts and learn to love deeper, harder and wider than we did before. I believe Love is what cradled, scooped, and carried me through the gravest loss of my life. And as such, the seeds of Love are sown fearlessly and flagrantly throughout this book.

We grieve because we have loved and lost. We heal through the work of grief and love.

And that is the heart and soul of *Lamentations of The Sea*: it is not a book about death, it is a book about Life and coming to realize Love in new ways through the living of loss. If the wound is the brokenness that comes from loss, our elixir is the transformative gifts of grief that come from learning to keep our hearts open and let Life bring new light in.

So grab a cup of cocoa. Take a quiet moment. Keep an open heart. Feel the places you bleed. Pull up a chair. Sit with me for awhile. Let's talk about the loving and the losing and the living. May you find warmth and healing in this space.

— BethAnne

Winter

GRIEF'S REACH

How far and long is the reach of grief: unwelcome, yet unwavering, in its temerity to stretch down deep inside of us and shine its light on the darkest of spaces.

1

How to Grieve

People will be willing to tell you what to feel, how to grieve, that you need to let go, but I have found at some point you are simply going to have to realize that People are not You.

And you are going to have to give yourself permission to make up your own rules.

You are going to have to come up with your own vocabulary for what you are feeling. Going to need to figure out what you need in order to grieve, going to have to define what letting go means to you. Maybe you want to redefine the entire concept of letting go so that it means you work on releasing yourself from everybody else's expectations, attitudes and values towards your grief, leaving you with the freedom to love and lose and grieve and rage and heal as you see fit.

Your grief then becomes an opportunity to test the boundaries and wander outside the lines. To feel beyond the grief models and books on loss and what worked for somebody else. Your grief then becomes an opportunity for you to make a break from anything that doesn't support your process and anyone who doesn't allow you space to determine your own needs.

Your grief then becomes a doorway to greater authenticity giving you the courage to own your experience and know it is valid. Your grief then becomes an invitation to show up for yourself, be your own source of wisdom, and turn that beautiful love that you give to others back upon yourself. Your grief then becomes the ultimate lesson on self-care, self-love, and self-healing. On listening to yourself.

And the best thing you can do for yourself is to create space to nurture the needs of your soul. It is a job that nobody can do for you, but you.

2

BLUE SYMPHONY

The ocean will teach you
many things if you let it.

How to cry like the waves…
all at once in
great gasps—
then a gentle slowing
that leaves salty pools of foam
at your feet.

How to see grief
like the pull of the tides
washing in
…and out…
in changing shades of
blue symphony.

How to stand still.
While life swirls on around you.
And how to keep moving
when life suddenly goes

still
— — —

I would give it this weight
if I could.
Let it float me down
to calmer shores,
but it tells me it is mine
to pull.

That we must learn
to bear the depths of
our own seas,
and realize how great
a weight our shores can learn
to hold and carry.

The ocean will teach you
many things,
if you let it,

The ocean will teach you
many things.

3

ELYSIUM

I go to sit on his favorite beach a few days after he died. Always sunny, turquoise waters, an endless blue sweep of sky; I try and feel my brother.

I believe there is an afterlife, that death is a door and not the end, but since he's been gone I can't see him, and I don't know how to open the door. For awhile I have no sense of him, but as I watch the waves go in and out, I consider that I am thinking too small. That he is BIG now—bigger in his After than he was in this Living. The spark of who he was as a human being, now a blaze of starlit flame.

That's when I realize that *he*, as I knew him with all of the struggles and woes and sadness he accumulated in this world, is no more. All of that has passed with him: the Old becoming New. And my brother is now Love, he is now Peace, he is now Compassion, he is now Forgiveness. He is part of the Light. In wonder, I gaze up into the sanctity of the sun and choose, in the infinite precision of that moment, to believe his spirit is happy and free.

I feel it then. A sense of a presence laughing joyfully on that beach. Young, carefree, riding the surf and giggling with glee. It is the most euphoric feeling I've ever know, like Elysium. I know he is there that day, cresting the waves, our old Dog by his side, churning up water and splashing about, telling me all is well. He stays there all afternoon with me on that beach. Surfing the stars, whipping the winds. Breezy, blithe, totally at ease.

And in that moment, I have no more questions about who or where or what he is: a Soul who has returned to Love. He surfs until the sun begins to set in the west, and it is time to leave for the day. He tells me he'll see me again. I cannot see him.

But I believe.

4

THE LONGEST WALK

This past weekend was my brother's memorial service and here is the good news on that: I will never have to relive that moment again, and every step forward is a step away from the rawest days of pain and loss.

*A*ll I know is that preparing for it felt like the emotional and spiritual equivalent of running 100 miles, and though I was sitting in the first row close to the podium, my walk to the front to give the eulogy was the longest, and the loneliest, walk I've ever endured. It is good that the podium was a thick wood stand since it hid the fact that my legs shook involuntarily and violently; I thought they might collapse from convulsion. They did not—I tried to scrunch my toes to keep me grounded, placed my hands on the top of the platform to keep me stable, took a big deep breath and began to speak the things I'd been carefully holding inside of me all week.

There are no words to describe the surreality of this experience: I only had one sibling, and now he is gone. I will never be in this position, ever again, saying these poignant, horrible words of goodbye. And there is no way I ever imagined I would be saying these words so soon, so young. I still say it multiple times a day, *I can't believe he's gone.*

I have learned that grief will set you apart on its own accord like a sorrowful sanctification process that hijacks you from the everyday stream of life and forces you into some nightmarish upside down grief land, which you have no choice but to find your way through. Up is down, and right is backwards, and forwards is usually impossible to find other than placing one foot in front of the other and taking one breath at a time.

I decided last week that since I am lost in Grief Land anyways, carried back to the past by memories of our life together, I may as well take advantage of the space and infuse each element of my brother's service with as much of him as I possibly can. So I labor over the words I write: polishing and shaping them again and again until they

7

seem to have perfect facets. I painstakingly piece together the video of his life, making sure I include all I can to show the brightness he possessed and the journey he took.

I am impeccable with the items I choose for the memory table and the pictures I have enlarged, along with the colorful weathered, wood frames I choose to display them. Then I wrap all of it up in invisible pink chords of healing, hope, and love that those who come might see something of the beauty in his life.

My brother was far from perfect—*and aren't we all?*—and since I believe in loving the whole and not just the sum of a person's best parts, I even figure out a way to include a little of his unpolished side in my words and give a nod to the fact that sometimes people's diamonds in the rough can be their own form of loveliness. But mostly I stick to the beautiful; memorials are for someone's light, not their dark.

I don't think I will ever forget standing up there, digging and reaching and finding the strength to keep my voice steady and true and clear, so I can let the ocean of words I speak wash over that audience of silent witnesses flowing in and out of people as they may. Sometimes you can't control or contain truth, you just let it go where it needs. In the end, I speak what I can of my brother's truth, in ways maybe even he couldn't have spoken for himself.

It is an honest, exhausting, bewildering tribute of love. And I hurt and relieve when it is over.

Yesterday I poured myself out, today I wake up feeling lighter than I have for the past few weeks. The sadness is still there, in spades and waves and unexpected outbursts of tears, but this sacred space I have been holding inside of myself in order to do this task—to speak well and true and through the eyes of love in front of a cloud of witnesses—this task is finished and that space has now been allowed to dissolve. It leaves me feeling freer and bigger, and in its dissolution, I realize the journey through Upside Down Grief Land continues.

Like my eulogy, I find there is no good way to end these words. At present, I'm not even close to the close—how can I possibly finish this essay when I can barely see the horizon on the edge of this strange, new, sorrowful land? So instead, I will close with the only words that have offered me any kind of close this week. They are the last words I spoke on my brother's behalf:

I didn't want to write the closing to this eulogy. Because writing a close means taking one more step closer to the reality that my brother's death is true. And that is a truth I simply do not want to be true. But in the end, I also know that death is just another journey. We open at the close. And this closure in my brother's life has opened him to new and beautiful things in the next.

Godspeed our friend, our son, my brother. May you forever rest in love and peace. And Brother Skywalker, may the force always be with you.

5

*The main task of grief
is trying to accept
and conceive of something that feels unacceptable
and inconceivable.*

6

BLANK SPACES

We don't always realize the spaces somebody fills in our lives.

*P*hysically, emotionally, mentally, energetically: we get used to arranging our gravitational orbit to accommodate their presence and learn to revolve in accord. We develop a unique emotional set point towards them, an imprint of feelings we only hold for that relationship. We form an introject in our mind that represents our thoughts, templates, and perspectives of them.

We create memories and stories and narratives about who they are and what they mean to us. We get used to them occupying all those spaces. Then one day they are gone, and there is nothing left but the void of empty space they once filled and a lingering sense of feeling lost at sea.

Loss will give you blank spaces, and you are going to feel lost for quite awhile, going to struggle with how to fill that empty space, how to *feel* that empty space. And it is going to become very important to give yourself both space and time to let life slowly help you find your footing again. Be kind and gentle to yourself as you do this. Something that was sacred feels ripped from you, and it's going to be awhile before Life forms itself around that void.

In the meantime, give it space to heal. And give yourself space to just be with it. Sometimes that is the best we can do—

Just allow the space for it to *be*.

7

CARRY YOU

My friend, My friend,
Oh where are you?
You went away, you left too soon.
The good we shared
I'll hold onto.

And in my heart, I'll carry you.

My brother, My brother,
Oh where are you?
Where there's now one, there once was two.
This song of grief
Sings clear and true.

And in my heart, I'll carry you.

My son, My son,
Oh where are you?
The love we have, naught can undo.
Our lives forever
Bound to you.

And in our hearts, we'll carry you.

Our love forever
Bound to you.

And in our hearts, we'll carry you.

8

BOUNCE

Today it feels like an endless lake of deep, blue sad. I'm stuck in the middle, sitting in a rowboat with no oars, dead in the water. The lake feels bottomless, but not quite endless, for somewhere out there I can see there is new land across the horizon, though I sense it's going to take awhile to reach.

*T*his lake I speak of is simply another landmark on a passage of grief I never expected to take. As I write these words, it has been exactly one month since my brother died, passing away from a medical condition we all believed was under control. He was my only sibling, and we were only one year apart—me 38, him 39. It is still unbelievable to conceive that one moment he was here and the next instantaneously gone, the fabric of my family and my life forever changing in that second.

Loss will bind you to an unwitting contract, signing you up for a one-way ticket across a wasteland of grief. You will find yourself plucked out of the trajectory you were traveling and deposited into uncharted territory, with ever changing terrain, that you must somehow learn to navigate without a map.

Some days it will be a barren desert, devoid of life, without relief in sight. Others, a stormy sea of whys and could have beens and all that was left unfinished and unsaid. And then you will find oasis for awhile, an unexpected cooling from the hot, salty tears that become a frequent occupant of your face. You believe you are starting to do okay… until a wave comes along and pulls you back into that crash of thrashing sea.

Mostly you feel like you are living somebody else's reality. You do your best to keep moving in the physical world that constructs *real life*, while inside you continue this invisible journey through a surreal and awful landscape, as you start to realize what you are experiencing inside feels more real than anything in the outside world.

At present, I have been sitting in my tiny boat in the middle of that vast, sorrowful lake for several days; the terrible tumult of the last four weeks starting to settle into my heart and mind and bones, making me aware of its finality and weight.

I am learning that death will change you. Grief will rearrange you. Loss will be an unexpected catalyst to a different version of self, and your process will not be understood by many. I have learned these lessons before through a painful divorce that marked a breaking and reconstructing of self; the passing of my beloved, and still missed, old faithful of a Dog; and a rapid series of betrayals and break-ups that left my heart broken and reeling.

It is with bittersweet irony that I have realized what has previously passed in my life has prepared me to make this particular journey. Emotional, mental and spiritual calisthenics that forced me to dig and reach and stretch to find my reservoirs of untapped strength. While this feels heavier, graver, and more terrible than the others combined, I know I can survive the passage. I just don't want to be here.

Those were the words I told my husband the day my brother died: *I just don't want to be here.*

After learning the news, we were frantically racing across town to get to my parent's house, and I told him that I knew the minute we got out of the car, crossed their threshold, and entered into a collective process of familial grief, that things were about to become real. I could already feel life snatching me out of the bounds of normal reality and placing me at the start of this wasteland of grief.

I had a felt sense of a giant mountain I needed to climb to gain entrance to grief's valley, and I remember telling him of that metaphorical mountain awaiting me and saying, *I know I have grown strong enough to climb it, to carry it… but I don't want to. I just don't want to be here.*

Here is where I find myself anyways.

There are many things we have a say about in our lives, but there are some things where we have no say. You can be walking along focusing on the path in front of you when you are completely blindsided by something you never predicted or saw coming. A tragedy, a trauma, a cataclysmic change that knocks you off that path, landing you in lonely, unexplored terrain where you are forced to become an inadvertent participant in a journey not of your making.

It is a journey of Life's making, and regardless of purpose or reason, you find yourself staring at that mountain wondering how you can possibly climb it, then somehow finding the courage to take that first step. There are days where you want to turn away and crawl back into the cocoon of normal that encapsulated life before all this happened. Days where you trick yourself into thinking you are further along than you really are, until pain once again demands attention, and you are reminded you are still a stranger in this strange land. Days where you search for short cuts and bailouts and time warps and learn the painful truth that the only way out is through.

There will be some people who understand the passage you take, for they too have walked these lands, but many will not. It is not their load to carry or their journey to make, and they will sit expectantly waiting for you to bounce back, waiting for you to reach that distant horizon, so life can resume as it once was. What they do not understand is that this is an unseen process of heart and spirit and soul, and you will not look the same upon its passage—there is no bouncing back.

We can't undo the strings of irrevocable change that are pulled when life turns upside down. We can't tie them back the way they were and return to the skin of self we previously wore. For better or for worse, we have been asked to step into a new version of self.

And if we allow it, grief holds the potential to shine a light on our soul. Stripping us of all the facades and pretenses that hide our authentic self. Revealing an untapped well of love, courage, and strength that awaits us in a time of darkest need. Helping us realize the intangible things that are most real while introducing us to our deeper, spiritual selves. Teaching us a new, resilient language of the heart that helps us become deeper, wider, and more than we were before. After its initial contraction, grief offers expansion—if we learn to let its light in.

I do not want to be here, on this small boat in this lamentable sea, but here I find myself anyway, doing my best to keep my heart open to the changes life is rendering inside. Time has become my best companion, reminding me that every step forward is a step away from that terrible mountain I first ascended and a step closer to that distant horizon, which still feels so far away.

But I believe there will come a day where I reach that place and find myself standing on new shore, and while things will never go back to the way I came, I know they weren't meant to. We didn't come here to stay the same, we came here so our hearts could be rearranged. Sometimes the best any of us can do is courageously take the journey Life hands us. Believe we will find our bounce again.

And learn to land wherever we may.

9

BREATHE

There are days it feels like I have been amputated, like half of my lungs have been ripped from my chest, it hurts so badly to breathe.

*A*nd the only thing that sustains and gives me breath is my fervent faith in the process of Life and my belief that Life holds the ability to resuscitate punctured lungs, if we can learn to breathe in something bigger than just ourselves.

And that's what I keep going back to when I grab for air within myself and cannot find it there: I have the breath of Life to fill my lungs, when I cannot fill them for myself.

And so it's one day at a time. One moment at a time. One breath at a time. Again and again. Over and over. As long as I need. Do this enough and you begin to realize:

A person can learn to breathe their way through anything.

10

HOW TO SWIM

There is a reason grief is often compared to the ocean.

*A*s you churn about in its watery grips, you can't help but know the strength of the sea. Where one moment you will be standing on the shore and the ground feels solid—you are making it through this, you are going to be okay. Then a rogue wave unexpectedly pulls you in, and you are floundering in the middle of the water, drowning for all you're worth... until you realize the ocean has spit you back out and you are once again on the shore. And though you don't know how you got there, there is solid ground beneath your feet.

While you can't stop the cataclysm that is grief when it comes, or keep yourself from being pulled into that tumult of an ocean, or ignore the difficult and necessary tasks that go along with caring for your heart after loss, you can choose how you go through it. You can choose to fill in the gaps and cracks and in between moments with as much self-compassion and kindness as you can. You can learn to let your giant heart and your fervent faith in the process of life be a lighthouse in your storm.

You can teach yourself how to swim in the watery depths by surrendering to the waves and letting them float and carry you for awhile, when you feel you can no longer carry yourself. And, even in the middle of the ocean, you can learn to take in life, look to the hope of the stars when you lose your way, and choose to let the one thing trying to pour from the seas of your heart flow:

A song of grief rising from the void in your deep.

11

The very thing that ails you
in this darkest of place
is the very thing
that will eventually see
you through to the light.

Love is both wound and balm.

12

And So I Lean

I spent today's gray and cloudy morning reorganizing old photos and albums. Keeping the ones that matter most, throwing away the others. There are many ones from my younger years, from my first marriage, that I smile at one last time before placing into the waste bin and letting them go.

*P*erhaps that sounds incredibly sad, but it isn't, not really. It is an exercise of love and compassion for my younger self, filled with a soft sense of nostalgia for the paths we travel in this life, which can look very different than expected and carry us far away from the places we started.

Life is a series of letting goes. A constant cycle of birth, death, and rebirth that evolves our relationship with ourselves and the world around us. It is a teacher who tells us to stop grasping so hard, open up our palms, and let what we cling to fall through our fingers, so life can place something new in our hands. When we learn to do this, we learn to lean into the rhythm of life and follow its flow instead of constantly fighting the current and trying to turn back the tides of change.

My grief has been so potent this week it feels like something is pressing down against my chest, squeezing the contents of my heart out and up as involuntary tears stream down my face. But even in this, even in this grief state and magnitude of loss, I am leaning. This is where Life has taken me, this is the flow right now.

And so I lean.

Most people fight our seasons of change. We don't want things to be different, we want them to stay as they were. We want what is already secure and knowable, and we fear the nebulous, future space of what we cannot see. Sometimes we cling to ideas, people, jobs, material things, our notions of how things should be, and our ideals of who we should be in an effort to fight the current and try to keep the order of life to our liking.

That was me 6 years ago. I had begun to realize that something was fundamentally wrong inside of me, inside of my marriage, inside of my heart and soul and fabric of being. Life is whispering, trying to tell me something, and I don't know how to listen. I bargain and compromise and try to create private pockets for myself to explore this crisis of spirit. Anything to keep the order of life as I know it.

I figure if I can negotiate with my spirit and patch myself up behind the scenes, I can fit myself back into the box of my life. I can go back to being the BethAnne that everybody knows and expects me to be. But all the while, the constructs I have built things on continue to tumble down inside, and there I stand among a landfill of crumbled hopes and dreams beginning to realize—I can't seem to fit things back into the box.

Five years ago, I finally laid my paltry compromises down at the feet of Life. And I learned to lean. That day will go down as one of the Top 10 Worst Memories of my life, and to this date, the single bravest, most authentic, heartbreaking, soul shaping decision I have ever made for myself.

After that, things were bad for awhile. A long while. But those are stories for another day, and what is important for this day is to share that there was hope in the midst of all the sorrow: hope for the possibility of what could be, hope for the possibility of something more, hope that Life was bigger than me, and therefore better suited to help order my life, so I could become the person I was meant to be.

There is beauty in the lean. A sense of rightness when we yield to Life and don't try and avoid or distract or dance away from the truths it is trying to impress upon our hearts. The lean is where we can begin to trust its process, even if we don't understand the direction we are going and can't see where our steps will take us.

I wrote an essay earlier this week that included the words, *We are not here to stay the same, we are here so our hearts can be rearranged.* I live by these words, have been living by them since that day 5 years ago when I agreed to let the current shape me, instead of trying to shape the current. My heart and soul and relationship to life and love have changed so much in this time that I have learned to hold nothing but grace and compassion for the girl I used to be.

We are who we are when we are younger. Doing out best to figure out this gorgeous, chaotic life, as we try and find our way through the days of the exterior world while discovering who we are in the scope of our interior world. We travel these lands by trial and error, our experiences becoming wise teachers who can take us to the deepest places in our hearts and help us find our own paths of truth when we learn to listen.

Two weeks ago my ex-husband came to the memorial service for my brother. We don't keep in touch, life has moved so far from where it once was, but he was there that day. He walked up to me after, introduced himself to my husband, gave me a hug, and told me he wouldn't have missed this service for anything: he once loved my brother also.

We spoke of life and the passage of time, his three children and wife, my recent marriage, and our plans to move to Kauai. At the end of it, I looked him in the eye, which may well have been for the last time, smiled and said, *You are exactly where you are supposed to be in life, aren't you?*

He kindly smiled back and said, *Yes, I believe I am.*

And I am too.

We can't always see the shape our days will take or know how Life will work things out. But we can learn to keep learning to let go. To let our loves, our losses, our griefs, our leans shape us. And we can always remember, no matter how unforeseeable the future may seem—

Life will not let you fall if you have the courage to trust it.

13

BYGONES

Leave them where
you last laid them down,
let them collect
the under use
of dusted decay.

Choose to love over them—
they never really mattered
anyway.

The only thing you take
with you is the contents
of your heart—

And hate is a heavy weight
to carry.

14

HURT

It's going to hurt for awhile. Hurt and hurt and hurt and hurt.

*A*nd my dear one, you're going to wish that it felt different, and it's going to go on hurting anyways. So when it comes? Those great gushes of grief, those masses of memories that sweep you back into another place and time, those awful waves of wist and want—

Set them free. Let them out.

Let yourself hurt like nobody's watching, because in the end, the only one you need to watch over is you. And right now?

You need to hurt.

15

OH BROTHER WHERE ART THOU

There is a place
not far from here
where there is no condemnation—
just grace.

Someday I will go
and meet you there.
But not yet,
not yet.

I look for you in blue skies
stretching ever on,
try to seek your whisper
in the crush of sea.
I believe I heard you in the whip
of night's wind:

But you've changed,
and I can't always find you.

There is a place
not far from here
where there is grace and no
condemnation.

Someday I will go
and we shall be free.
But not yet, my brother.

Not yet.

16

HEART

Sometimes you just have to feel it.

*L*et the natural expression of pain flow, which honors the strength it takes to try for love. The absolute courage it requires to tangle your heart with another and risk the words "I love you." Risk vulnerability, risk hurt, risk all the unknowns that may come your way. Risk the potential loss that may someday hit with unexpected suffering.

There is no shame to be found in having a hurting heart when your hopes haven't gone as planned and life has brought you to a point of break. No shame at all. Your heart is doing what it is built to do: *love, feel, break, heal.*

The human heart is one of the most achingly fragile and sturdily resilient forces on the planet. Don't be afraid of what it has to say. Don't be afraid of its depths. And don't be afraid to let it do what it needs to do to *release, remember, repair, renew.*

We contract so we can expand. It is the only way a heart knows to grow.

17

SEAS OF INFINITY

Back when we were young
we used to catch fireflies in jars and call it magic.
We roamed the space of unstoppable
while our dreams swam the seas
of infinity.

They say there is a certain
order to this world:
The dawn of day is supposed to be
followed by dark of night.
The rush of spring preceded
by the still of fall.
And the child is not meant to
say goodbye before the parent—
death is no home
for the young.

Back when we were young,
we tied capes round our necks
and believed we could fly to the sky.
We laughed at the nonsense of rain
and built lands
of hope and silly putty.

They say that no matter,
things carry on:
The sun will still rise with soft morn.
The health of summer always relieves
a winter's harsh heart.
And time will change
the shape of the wound—

so one can better see
the grace of light.
Back when we were young,
we ruled the forests
of Hyrule as King and Queen.
We believed everything was possible
and ate breakfasts of wishes
and fancy.

They say that Life has a rhythm
all its own:
The moon will keep
dance with the tides.
The force that is Love will forever
remain the greatest mystery.
And there will be some things
we do not understand—
we're asked to keep faith,
anyways.

My Brother, My Brother,
may you find peace in those
seas of infinity.
We were unstoppable.

Back when we were young.

18

THE GRACE OF BEING

for Sarah, you are the bravest soul I've ever known

You love how you love. You hurt how you hurt. You grieve how you grieve. You heal how you heal. These are the words I wrote to a friend who is also going through grief. She seems to be in judgment of her own process, thinking she should be doing better than where she currently finds herself.

Most of us know what it feels like to be this person; we often judge our own process and expect ourselves to be in another space, a better space, than where we find ourselves to be. I know how it feels to be this person, because I have been this person off and on these past few weeks, expecting myself to be at a different point in my grieving process than I actually find myself.

Once again, I continue to learn that it actually takes tremendous courage and self-compassion to look yourself squarely in the eye, acknowledge where you are standing, then allow yourself to be in that space: no judgment attached. At present, my process has more to do with being than with doing, which is uncomfortable for many people. In Western culture, doing is equated with progress, wellness, and moving forward, while being is equated with wallowing, stagnation, and staying stuck.

Doing is climbing mountains and going for runs to shift my energy. Doing is writing these words as an act of catharsis. Doing is going out, pretending to be present with others, successfully making it a quarter of the time, while the other three quarters fills itself with a considerable echo in my head—*my brother is dead, my brother is dead, my brother is dead*—as the absurdly, casual conversation of life swirls on around me.

Being is what happens at 3 a.m. Being is awakening from sleep each night, remembering the surreality of your reality and finding the clench of sorrow inside your guts still twisting and turning.

Being is staring off into space—breathing, seeking, searching—and sitting with your present state of soul. Being is done with an intentional stillness, allowing whatever one feels to wash over them in wave after wave.

Being is what transforms the soul. Doing is simply what comes next.

As with many things, when it comes to matters of the heart and soul in our culture, we've got it backwards. We honor and elevate the productivity of doing, while minimizing and missing the grace of being. But the truth is, we often receive more spiritual growth and development, more truths of the heart, more clues to our authentic nature in our moments of being than in the ones of productivity.

I have intuitively known since Brent passed that what will most support my process is going to be found in the quiet gathering of being, rather than the energy expenditure of doing. Most days I find myself making space to intentionally sit with my sadness, as I believe there is great purpose in sadness right now, though it would be easy to miss if you haven't learned to be open to sorrow's gifts.

Sorrow is its own form of intelligence. Sorrow becomes the teacher who teaches us how to reach for light. Sorrow becomes the teacher who teaches us that pain is the gateway to love. Sorrow becomes the teacher who reminds the wounded healer: we heal ourselves so we can better offer healing to others.

Sorrow becomes the teacher who reminds us there are many things that are broken, which cannot be fixed. Nor were they meant to be. It is not our job to mend the bent wing of every wounded bird. It is Life's hope and Love's calling that we simply learn to fill the space around that broken wing with love and believe in its ability to find its own means of healing. This is an act of true connection, powerful beyond measure, and it always lets another be exactly where they are at.

We love how we love. We hurt how we hurt. We grieve how we grieve. We heal how we heal.

I met a friend for lunch yesterday. She walked in and gave me a book of poetry by Hafiz; looked me in the eye and said how much she loves me and loves my brother, for even though she never met him, she, like me, believes we are all connected; then proceeded to hug me and say how beautiful I am to her in my sadness. In this time, she is one of few who has truly seen there is beauty in this darkness, love in these ashes, the origins of new life in my grief.

And that every drop of sorrow I feel is simply a drop in the greater ocean of love.

Courage comes in all shapes and forms. They say sometimes it roars, but I think its biggest roar is the simple act of being present with another in their pain. Or better yet, being present with yourself in your pain. Don't turn away from it. Don't look aside. Do not distract yourself and miss this chance to grow your heart in exponential form. Just learn to BE with it. And trust Life to take care of the beauty of your becoming.

That is my gift of being right now. Allowing this pain space in my life. Letting it wash into me in great waves when I hurt. Letting it wash out of me in great waves when I suffer. Offering those waves to Life on behalf of all those who hurt and suffer. But most of all, offering them for those who are blind to their own hurt and suffering. May they find the Courage to break. May they find the Love to heal their broken wings. May they realize there is nothing more that Life wants than for us to discover our ability to fly, because that is what I find in the middle of my waves: breaking and loving and living and mending.

I love as I love, I hurt as I hurt, I grieve as I grieve, I heal as I heal.

19

THE MISSING

I miss him.

Not in the, "I miss you, let's catch up," kind of way that you miss a friend when you haven't connected in awhile. Not in the longing kind of way you experience where someone you love lives in a different state, and you yearn to see them. This is more like a missing in action, punch to the gut, "where did you go and why did you have to leave?" kind of miss. Like I keep searching for him among the pieces of daily life and keep realizing over and over and over again… he is nowhere to be found.

I miss him so much the missing often feels like weights around my ankles, a giant backpack of loss strapped to my shoulders that nobody can see except the one who bears its weight, and some days I hate how great a weight it is to carry.

I am learning as I go—as I look back and see I have traveled many miles, even with the weights of this constant, dreaded pack—to carry it. I am learning that missing someone doesn't prevent you from moving forward and seeking new ground. I am learning how to take this hole in my heart and plant a tree there, which reaches high up to the stars, so I can climb the branches to the top and better reach my brother. I am learning just how strong we can be when asked to carry the full of who we are. I am learning that some aches and pains will stay with us forever, and we should wear them as badges of honor that say—I was *here* and this mattered.

And I am learning, that even as my voice calls out into the wilderness searching fruitlessly through the night, that if I still myself—get out of my head and drop into my heart—I will find he is still with me, hidden deep inside.

20

TAKE A KNEE

for Dad

There are three things
in this life I will never forget:

The sound that is the
sad lamentation of the sea.
That spaghetti was
my brother's final supper.
And the sight of my father
kneeling before his fallen son,
weeping.

Take a knee.

For those who suffer
silent grief.
Let your heart be opened
by their stories untold.
Let it rearrange you,
this finite sense that's loss—
and when your sorrow comes…
still life for awhile,
and take a knee.

There are a few more things
I wish I could have said:

That I'm sorry for the one time
with your chocolate cake
when I said I just wanted a "bite."

How I thought it was really cool
the way you couldn't be anybody
other than yourself.
And that I always loved you,
even when we were unlovable,
and I wish you could
have felt that.

Take a knee.

For those who stumble
in the dark.
Learn to walk in shadow
to better know your light.
Don't be afraid of pain of soul
it's how our spirits grow—
and when your own pain comes…
gain it entrance,
and take a knee.

There are some things
I must do to honor
your journey of life:

I promise to always keep
your green lightsaber close by.
I will take good care
of Mom and Dad per your last request.
And learn to live for both of us,
and hold you as I go.

Take a knee.

For those who go
too soon.
Honor what has come to pass
by living well and true.

Learn to keep them in your heart
for love lives on and on—
and when your memories come...
cherish them,
and take a knee.
And when your sorrow comes...
still life for awhile.

And take a knee.

21

START

My life feels like an old car trying to start some days.

I keep turning the key, pressing the accelerator, hearing sounds that it's going to get going, until it sputters and once again goes quiet. It has occurred to me that maybe what I need is a new car, and I completely understand why some people make drastic changes to their lives after a major loss. Is is achingly difficult, maybe even impossible, for some to pick up their threads and keep on going. They need new threads so they can try and start over.

New threads or not, life doesn't stop just because of grief, this world will keep on spinning, churning out new patterns around you. It is both comforting and disconcerting: things carry on, even as you find yourself standing in motion, stuck in a perpetual good-bye, keeping time to the dull rhythm of pain's beat. Some days I find I am able to unstick and spin with it, and some days I find myself stopping, pausing, and trying to curl up deep inside where the fray of it all doesn't feel so frayed.

It is like grief is dissolving something within, and the constructs that compose my life have turned pale and foggy and fragmented. I keep trying to gather myself into me only to find parts of myself keep slipping through my fingers, and the only thing I can find to glue myself into some semblance of togetherness right now is the permission to not be okay. To not know. To dissolve. To sputter. To not start. To lose myself. To wait in the face of change.

To let life spin out around me as I stand still in grief's space of nothingness, until I find my threads of self again, figure out a way to pick them up and weave them into a resolution. Find what I need to turnover and hear the sounds of a start.

22

True inner peace
isn't contingent on stability, happiness,
and everything going the way
we expected.

Instead, the peace
we cultivate inside ourselves
is contingent on our ability
to let go and give
Life permission
to shape us.

23

FOR LUCK

I've started calling them Brent pennies and collecting them in a cup as a symbol of love and luck.

*I*t's not unlike me to stumble upon signs and symbols that are personally meaningful and interpret them as a reminder from Life that I am not alone. I find hearts all the time, see 11:11 at least once a day, have butterflies fly across my path, and often find the symbols of the rose and rainbow in the most unusual places.

But a penny has never been one that I connected with until recently.

It began the week before my brother passed when I had a series of bizarre dreams. A bobcat leading me through the darkness to safety. Strange star beings pressing a triangle on my forehead and trying to communicate with me. Two midnight black ravens on the windshield of a wrecked car, one of them bloody and dying, the other with a big red heart on her chest weeping and wailing over the loss of her love.

This was the week that I had the impulse to watch the movie *Ghost*, though I hadn't seen it in years. It's hard not to tear up when Sam proves he's real to Molly by moving a penny up the wall and floating it over to her. "For Luck," he says.

The day before my brother died, I was in the airport getting ready to board the plane for Kauai. *Unchained Melody* came on the overhead speakers reminding me of the movie we just watched. "Hey, it's Ghost!," I excitedly said to my husband. And right at that moment, I looked down, and there was a brand new shiny penny laying at my feet. We remarked on the strange synchronicity and the bizarre dreams of my week, and we wondered at the meaning.

I kept that penny. It is currently sitting in a jar on my nightstand along with a tiny scrap of paper that has the words, "For Luck." And now whenever I find a penny, especially during those times I am feeling most low and thinking of my brother, I pick them up and keep them.

Brent pennies. I will take comfort in whatever form it comes.

Strange things have been happening since he passed. Sometimes I hear him in my mind like he's speaking to me. I suppose it would be easy to dismiss that as figments of my imagination, but they're not my thoughts; they are more like text messages that just appear in my awareness. Words of encouragement for me, instructions on something to tell Mom and Dad.

Another evening the lights flickered, my television turned off for no reason, and I had the most pressing urge that Brent wanted me to contact my mother. So I did. Turns out she had been crying all night and praying for a sign that Brent was safe and well. *I think I'm your sign Mom. The only reason I checked in with you is because I felt like Brent wanted me to.*

There have been all sorts of other oddities. Music disappears off my phone, *Hello* and *Halo* are the songs missing most frequently. After three rounds of discovering these songs are gone when I go to listen to them, I have learned they always show back up the next day.

I have a blue heart shaped stone that I bought after his passing for remembrance, which always sits on my nightstand. Yesterday morning I went to get coffee and found it had moved from my stand to my pillow. Nobody else was in the house.

And most recently, a picture showed up on my phone of a brilliant, turquoise-blue light. Sandwiched between pictures of the desert mountain I was hiking that day is a photograph of a glowing blue orb on my camera roll. I couldn't tell you how it got there, it just showed up: there are many spiritual traditions that believe turquoise is the color of the Soul and the color that represents the highest form of Spirit.

Last weekend I was in Sedona, Arizona with a friend, taking a quick get away to get some sunshine and warmth for my tired heart. On our trip, I decided to go see a psychic named Roz who I chose, because her name and picture felt friendly and warm. I didn't go see her so she could tell me my future—I believe she could speak to the possibilities of the future, but I don't believe most of the future is set in stone. Our choices determine the course that comes next.

I just wanted to find out my possibilities. To see how they resonate with my own intuitive sense. Which is how I find myself sitting in an office filled with inspirational quotes, a fluorescent picture of Jesus, angel figurines, and an amethyst crystal ball. Roz is kind and welcoming, and as soon as I sit down she immediately starts speaking:

You're a healer.

Yes, I say.

You have a tremendous gift, but you're out of balance. There is so much sadness in you.

Yes. My brother recently died.

You have strong gifts of clairvoyance and you hear things in your mind.

Yes, I reply. *Though I do not think of myself as such—perceiving and having words and pictures pop in my mind has been normal since childhood. I never attached a label beyond intuition.*

You feel constrained in life, boxed in.

Yes. I've been a Psychologist for almost 15 years, but there is so much more that I want to do with healing work in addition to that.

You would make an excellent Psychic. You have all the gifts.

I laugh.

And this is the part where you should laugh too and insert joke about the girl who goes to a Psychic, who tells her she has a future as a Psychic. And the best part is—she didn't see that one coming.

You were born to do this if you choose.

I smile. *The Psychologist who became a Psychic. It makes a good story*, I say.

So our time goes. And as she says many other things, she pauses to tell me she senses another being, that I am not alone in the room. A male presence. Stubborn. Standing at my back, pushing me to become all I can. *He knows your gifts*, she says. *He is not going to give up on pushing you to use them.* This is the third person—all parties independent of one another—who has had an image of the spirit of my brother standing behind me. Bracing my shoulders and giving me strength, as I brace and give strength to those I help on my path.

And lately, that path has included even more curious phenomenon than usual. I am beginning to get used to it, having finally understood that such things are not easily understood with the western mind, which has been trained all too well in logical, rational thinking. Better to understand with the heart, who seems to know the language of beyond and realizes that anything is possible.

Today was one of those low days where I felt like a refugee coming out of some terrible grief war, seeking safety and peace and struggling to find them. I came home from work and saw the chart of my brother's star laying on the kitchen table. There was a shiny penny sitting right on top.

For Luck.

24

THE THICK

If you are in the thick of it, please tread kindly with yourself.

*G*rief is a confusing and jagged process; loss creates a sense of internal lawlessness that knows no rules or bounds. Your psyche devolves into disarray as the constructs and schemas you have built your sense of reality on tumble down, obliterated. What you believed to be true turns on its head, and it's so mentally disorienting it is difficult to know which way is up. Gravity doesn't exist in the thick of grief.

The way you once saw the world becomes an ideological pile of debris you are forced to sort. Your neural networks turn into traffic jams and dead end roads and abrupt cliffs of irresolution, while you search for the answer of what it means for someone to cease. And you begin to find that the model of grief you are living is one where every stage is mixed together, an emotive mass of finger paints with a tiny dot in the middle that says: "You are here."

You are *here*. And that is the good news, because it means you are still going. Still finding a way to swim through molasses, walk through quicksand, put one foot in front of the other, even though you're floating untethered in space. And while it is a sticky and messy process, one without a time limit or rulebook, you are still going, still breathing, still trying to show up.

I'd reach through these pages and give you a hug and a gold star for doing that much if I could. This may be the hardest thing you will ever endure and have to drag yourself through. Your gravitational orbit will never look the way it did before, and it's going to take your brain and your body and your heart some time to undergo reconstruction, rebuild, and repair.

In the meantime, go gently on yourself for you are in the thick, and you are still moving. Which means you are doing beautifully, you wonderful, brave human.

25

REACH

I am beginning to learn that the reach of grief stretches far.

*I*t has now been a little over two months since my brother passed away, and my days have become vivid lessons in what it means to be human, what it means to love, and what it means to undergo an emotional, mental, and spiritual journey of loss and heartache.

Some days feel so dark that I find myself composing letters to Life that go something like this: *Dear Life. You can be so horrible sometimes. Fuck you!* Other days, the light breaks through in unexpected patterns of grace, and I find myself writing different kinds of words: *Dear Life. You can be so beautiful sometimes. Love you!*

For the record, though the former feels pettily satisfying to write, ultimately I believe the later is a better approach. Love is always the answer, as its message of hope cannot help but transform a space when it's allowed entrance. Believing that however, still does not circumvent the process of feeling the anguishing stuff of life.

To grieve is to know anguish, and anguish lingers. Like an initial head cold that drops down into your chest and settles in for a long, raspy, reoccurring bout of bronchitis, I have come to realize how deep and long is the reach of grief. How much my chest and bones and cells are still struggling to find clean, clear breaths in its presence.

I have also come to realize over these weeks how much we as a culture have little idea on what to do with loss and grief. People look to the one grieving to take the lead, to tell them when they're better, to give them directions on what's okay to say. I watch people struggle to know what to say to me, often avoiding the topic altogether for fear of somehow making it worse.

I finally told a group of friends: *Look, everybody is afraid of saying the wrong thing so they say nothing. Let me set the record straight—there is nothing you can say that is going to make this more wrong. Nothing you can do that is somehow going to make this worse. What's wrong and worse for me, or for anyone who has loss, is that the person they love is gone. You can't make that worse more worse by an honest expression of care. Bringing it up isn't going to break them. It's probably going to help them.*

I have wondered how many other people have suffered a tragic loss and found silence from people where solace should be. Have had the experience of people not asking them how they are doing, of tip toeing around the topic, of only talking about surface things, because they assume you don't want to talk about it, or they are uncomfortable with the topic themselves, or they don't want to make you sad.

Except you are sad. And you do want to—*need to*—talk about it. Your loss came with such glaring magnitude that it left gaping breaks in the fault lines of your heart, and pretending like those don't exist feels so disingenuous that it makes it worse. I want to tell people that it's okay to ask me. It's okay if I'm sad. It's okay if you don't have the right words or don't know what to say or do—I don't expect you too. It's just that most of the time I don't have the energy to tell you all this, because I'm reaching with all my might, trying to claw my way through the pain. But that doesn't mean I don't need to know that somebody else is willing to be present and reach with me for awhile.

Somewhere along the way our culture has developed serious misconceptions about how life should look that limit the way we relate to ourselves and limit our ability to support one another in authentic ways. Problems, hardships, and tragedies often get minimized and reduced to something that needs to be cheered up, contained, or fixed. When often these are the very ingredients that provide a gateway for growth of the heart, spirit, and soul.

Life wasn't meant to be lived as a linear ideal, where we live in perpetual states of positivity, good mood, and curative thinking. Life was meant to be lived as a whole. We have emotions so we can experience the entire spectrum of feelings. Acknowledging both the dark and light is what it means to be human. Integrating the beautiful and the horrible and finding the lessons that come from both is at the core of being whole.

We make mistakes so we can learn. Good things can come from what seemed bad. Bad things can come from what seemed good. We learn from both and through those lessons, experience becomes our teacher of truth. Self-knowledge our teacher of authenticity.

Loss is a profound teacher, and it is part of the whole of life. It is important for us to learn to be present with our self and with others in the face of grief and loss. There are tremendous lessons of growth that can be found in such a space. Like how the essence of love keeps no score, giving of itself graciously and freely. Like how any offering of kindness, empathy, and compassion towards one another is a healing balm for the ruptures that have formed in the cracked foundation of this world.

Like the sense of grace and acceptance that can come when you realize you are doing the best you can with horrible circumstances. It helps you realize the same holds true for others—we are all just doing the best we can on any given day. Our job isn't to judge our process, but to embody our lives even when we find ourselves in hard places.

Many days I wake up, and I don't like the place I find myself. While I know life won't always be here, it is here now, and I know I choose to show up for myself and be present with my experiences. I choose to embody this strange space of grief that has already irrevocably changed and continues to transform me.

On the awful days I try and practice radical self-compassion, *It's okay to ache how I ache when and where I ache*, I'll say. I try to let my soul curl into life and allow myself to be supported by something bigger than myself. I have found that the world can hold you in a stasis of comfort if you let yourself be still.

And on the days where the sky breaks, where I feel my brother in the warmth of the sunshine, where I hear his voice among the shifting clouds, and I see faint hopeful traces of the pattern that is composing the threads of my days—

On those days I lift my chin up to the light, stretch my arms out to the sky. And I reach.

26

The biggest truths in Life
never are black and white.

They are found in holding
the sum of two opposing truths side by side
and acknowledging they both have a place in
the whole of our hearts.

My heart grieves. And it loves.
Profusely.

27

SUNSHINE IN WINTER

Beautiful things can come from an immense space of darkness.

$\mathcal{I}$t is my observation that most people value the beautiful, the light, the sunshine, while missing the value that darkness has in helping us break and grow and stretch in ways we never did before. There was a reason when I created a blog that I called it *Sunshine in Winter* and not just *Sunshine*. For I have found the Winter part is just as important as the Sunshine if you want to learn to shine bright in this world.

Winter is our losses. Winter is our heartbreaks. Winter is what happens every time we put on our Charlie Brown ghost sheets, optimistically head out the door to go trick or treating, and Life throws stones into our bag leaving us shouting, "No fair! I got a rock!"

Winter is what we do with those rocks. The times we cry over them, grieve over them, suffer over them, and then learn all we can from them. Learn to face them, examine them, tend to them. Mine them for all they are worth. Hold them up to the light then polish them, so they become diamonds of darkness that make our lights brighter.

Winter is where I learned to carve out a holy space inside of myself and fill it with the things that nourish my soul. Love and bravery and finding the courage to do the right thing every time my heart knew the right thing to do. Peace, connection, kindness, and the belief that we are all standing around the same sphere looking at it from different points of views, and the sum of that is called humanity.

I filled that space with what is sacred and what is mundane, having learned that magic is found in the simplest of places starting with our ability to take a breath and experience love. I filled it with the idea that life is a gift, and we are here to experience, care for, and tend to this gift in the ways that call to each of us. We are here to savor life and find our light, even in times of sorrow.

And every night I kneel in this holy space, light a candle for my brother, and let the love I hold towards him strengthen me. Remind me of what is most important in this world. Remind me what it means to be real.

Winter is where we find the truth of our soul. Sunshine is simply what comes from that.

28

SONGS OF THE TREES

Life can be terribly fragile;
they say to live it with
no regrets.

But how do you live
with another's regrets…
all those mets
not met?

The trees will tell you,
there are no perfect lives.
We plant our roots
as best we can
and no matter how
gnarled and twisted,
try to stretch
for the sky.

In the end,
we can't unmake
what has been made;
we can only be as the trees
and find a way,
in the fragility
of this place,

To keep our feet grounded.

Then faithfully move
in the direction
of the light.

Grief's Rebirth

Grief will plunge you into madness, and it is easy to get lost in this space. But never forget there is always a calm on the heels of the storm; the birth of new spring after winter's cold face; and chaos, in all its black mantle of dark and glorious eruption of light, will always precede new creation.

29

Our responsibility
to ourselves is not to deny
the internal damage done to the lands where pain
and grief exists,
but to embrace the
wounds of the land,
then learn to cover them with
new life and new love.

30

RELATIONSHIPS

You will find as you go through grief that there are two groups of people in this world.

*T*here are the people who have suffered terrible loss that hit so close to home they feel forever punctured with the wound. These are the people whose hearts are right there with yours whenever they hear of your loss: their own experience is so visceral and permanent, they know exactly what it is to be at those early stages of the grieving process.

Then there are the other people who have yet to lose someone close to them. So they don't understand the scope of grief. It's like trying to explain the subtleties, nuances, and shades of colors to someone who has been color blind their entire life. It simply doesn't transmute.

And within the group of those who haven't experienced loss, there are two more kinds of people. There are the ones who have known pain, hardship, and suffering in other forms in their lives, so they know the pain of grief. The ones who have these giant, compassionate, connected hearts that are so open to imagining how it feels, that they offer comfort, patience, and kind words with extreme sensitivity and tender care.

Then there are the ones who just don't get it. For a variety of reasons. Some of them have good intent but won't have the experience base or the emotional range that comes from that experience, until it is their turn to go through a magnitude of loss someday. Some of them don't want to come anywhere close to the pain, so they avoid it and, in so doing, avoid you to avoid getting near to sadness. And for some, death is just too scary and real a topic to confront—too much of a reality check that nobody is getting out of here alive.

The truth is that death will show you exactly where people are at in life. It will show you where you are at. Where your family is at. Where your friends are at. Where your community is at. Where your culture is at. It will teach you about emotional availability and a person's capacity to face pain square on—in their relationship with their own self and in their relationship with others, for our ability to be emotionally available to others is only as deep and wide as our ability to be emotionally available to ourselves.

And it will rearrange some of your relationships. Old friendships may change—some for the better, some for the worse. New friendships may arise. You may be surprised by who supports you and surprised by who doesn't. You may feel supported. You may feel hurt. You may feel isolated. You may feel horribly alone in the thrash of your grief. You may receive incredible light from unexpected sources.

Whatever you feel and experience in your relationships, just know that it is okay to take a deep breath, gives things space, and let them rearrange as they need. Your priority right now is to try and show up for yourself, to learn to be your own best friend who nurtures *you* through this loss. To be present with your feelings and lovingly remind yourself that your experience is right and true and valid. To give space where things need space and trust it will all work out as it should.

And you will find that when it comes to the people in your life, those who are meant to stick will absolutely stick. And those who have a little growing to do will do a little growing, and, when and if the time is right, return to your life again. And for those who get weeded out, who were only meant to go on the journey so far with you but are unable to make this part, because it feels too big or scary or unknown for them—release them.

We are not always meant to hold each other's hands forever: sometimes just long enough to see each other through a certain passage until we are forced to let go. And in the meantime, this is a very good opportunity to go about the work of learning to hold your own hand, listening to your heart, and honoring what it has to say.

31

PLASTIC HORSES

Trying to control
grief is like trying to
chorale the Wild West
with a toy sheriff badge
and a squirt gun.

My best defenses fall
like plastic horses.

Grief's stampede renders
chaos unordered.

32

STARLUCK

Lately, I have often thought that if I had a time machine, I would zip ahead 6 months in the future. I don't need to go too far, the purpose of life is to live it not skip it, just far enough to get me away from this present space.

Things seem to be at an aching plateau right now. I had an awareness this week that I feel obliterated. Like some part of my heart has been decimated. And as each passing week goes by, my awareness of the damage and casualties just keeps growing. I just can't seem to wrap my mind around the fact that my only sibling, the person I shared the same womb with, just dropped over one day. Medical explanations aside, how is somebody suddenly gone like that? That singular event hasn't just been a sadness or pain or bad season in life, it's been an annihilation of someone I loved.

And it still feels unacceptable.

This is what denial looks like by the way: it's not an intentional—just stay distracted and pretend *I'm fine*—kind of denial, it's involuntary. Here on its own accord. Putting a barrier up inside my brain that keeps some part of me from accepting this fact as an acceptable event on my timeline.

It makes me want to travel back to my self of 9 weeks ago in my little shiny time machine, bring that girl hot soup and warm cookies, and give her a big hug. She's going to need a lot of warmth and fortitude in the months ahead, and I know she could use comforting. *Be gentle on yourself,* I would tell her. *You have no idea what you're about to walk into.*

It makes me want to keep on zipping around from there and zip back to anyone I may have ever failed to fully support in loss, bring them containers of hot soup and warm cookies and giant hugs, and tell them how brave they are for still getting up each day and trying to keep moving. *I know you're going to need hot soup for a long time,* I'd say. *I'm here to bring you a cup whenever you need and will sit as close or as far away as you want. I believe in you. I am here for you. No expectations.*

I simply didn't know how wretched in heart this kind of loss feels. As well prepared as I thought I was to face it, I find that I have never felt anything like it. As I told someone recently: this new dead brother version of reality sucks.

I like to imagine that future me is looking back and sending all the love she can to this present version of self. *I know you can do this,* she says. *I believe in you. Help is on the way!* Future self has already learned the lessons I am currently learning. Her heart has already undergone the reconstructive surgery I am currently undergoing. She knows how this chapter will end and how the next one will begin. She knows the beauty that will come from the ashes of this time.

Future self has seen enough of the timeline go by that she is able to derive some meaning and purpose for her life from all that is currently transpiring. She sees how deep the roots of peace and compassion have grown in her Tree of Life. She knows how to be one serious Bad-Ass-Rainbow-Ninja-Warrior-Of-Love. She has borne witness to the beautiful pain of her own becoming, and she knows how to stand tall.

She is standing in the space of Spirit that exists beyond the physical bounds of land and time, and she is pulling on the chord of my soul, gently helping me move through this horrible time. *C'mon,* she says, *I know you can do this.* She's not giving up, and when the pulling is a little extra hard, she finds my brother pulling beside her.

They are Spirit Pirates, Captain and First Mate, sailing their ship, *Starluck,* around the Seas of Infinity. They see they've got a crew member drowning, and they are helping pull her along with all their might. And even though girl overboard can't see them, they see her. There is no other place they need to be than helping her right now. They have all the time in the world, because that concept doesn't exist in Spirit Pirate Land. Time is infinite. Space is infinite.

So is love, and they give it to her in spades. Sending it to her so strongly that it crosses the time-space barrier, and she somehow feels it fall through the sky and land with a soft thud on her heart, when she is beginning to lose it and most needs support. *We believe in you. We are here for you. No expectations,* they say.

Nine weeks down, and I can genuinely say that I never saw any of this coming. Not just losing Brent, but the grief trigger that got pressed when he passed. The complete chaos and disruption it's creating in my life. The inability to keep going as I have been; to pick up the threads that used to compose the structures that built my life and the fabric that built my identity.

I told a friend yesterday who asked me what I needed, that *this* was what I needed. We were having wine at her house, and she was listening, letting me tell my untold stories of my brother, of my grief, of all the horrible I'm holding right now. *I just need a witness. A friend. Somebody who will listen without judgment. I need quiet spaces, and mountains, and bowls of soup. Just be with me. Let me be ugly human. Be present with me for just awhile. I feel so empty. I need.*

A full moon shone bright, couple bottles emptied, stories witnessed and told; we talked long into the night.

33

BECOMING

Loss can take you to some dark places.

Places you don't want, but can't help to go. Places marked by despair and great pain, anger, and a sense of senseless want. Places where it is hard to hang onto silver linings or fragile hope or any sense that the sun will shine again. These are the places where you may encounter what feels like the very worst of yourself.

A time may come when you begin to miss the old you: the you you were before this awful loss. And you want to squeeze back into that old shell of self—take your old problems back, take your old sense of normal back. Take back the luxury of not having to live with the heavy press of grief.

A time may come when you look in the mirror, and you don't like what you are becoming.

But that's just it, isn't it? You ARE becoming.

All this awful, nasty, sticky mess is part of the passage of grief and holds the potential to help shine a light into our darkest spaces, where we will be forced to face our own debris. Forced to find ways to dig deep and bring a blaze of bright into our own darkness. Forced to find the stars that help us navigate this night.

This is the place where we learn to expand. This is the place where we learn Love is big enough to love over our most miserable parts of self. This is the place that holds the potential for incredible heart growth. This is the place where we come face to face with ourselves and find—

We are always stronger than we think we are, always have a little bit more to give than we think we do, and are always filled with an infinite supply of grace to see us through the journey.

34

RAGE STAGE

There is a crazy person
inside my head
screaming, screaming, screaming
with all her might.
Some days I feel I must kill
this girl who's crazy before she
kills the girl who used
to be me.

35

SAHARA

These past few weeks the wheels are falling off. I feel like Maximus in his chariot, careening wildly, surrounded by peril on all sides of the arena, trying to keep control of this beast of burden. Except the peril is my psyche, the chariot my grief, and both are in utter pandemonium.

*T*his week has felt like waking up from some horrid, alternate reality version of life and then discovering all over again just how real the past two months have been. There is this little girl, some younger part of myself who has yet to make her voice heard, emerging in my head and screaming, "I didn't even get to say goodbye. Didn't have any warning. Never got to see my brother one last time." She is fixating on how he died—one moment there, the next not—because that seems impossible to her.

She can't fathom *gone*.

On a March day where it is grimy and gray and grim outside, I feel equally ashen within. Annihilated and bereft. Completely broken by this loss. I thought I was coping with it and moving through, that the worst part, those initial few weeks, was over. But it has hit anew.

It feels like it just happened again, and I am standing at the desert's edge, my own vast, forsaken Sahara of Grief, and I have no choice but to cross, if I ever want to move out of this terrible space. I am ill equipped. Unskilled. Inept. I try and begin the journey only to get beaten back by the elements, as I realize how vast is nature and how little am I.

I knew this was going to be bad. Remember that horrible weight that attached itself to me the moment I learned of my brother and knew that Life had just signed me up for a passage I never wanted to take. But I didn't know how bad or how long or how strong the windstorms, which come sweeping through my interior flattening and scattering and dismantling everything they cross, would be.

I can't go back, and most days I don't know how to go forward, and I'm having it out with Life over it all. I'm being cracked apart again, and I have rage. It's not the first time Life has pushed me off the safety of wall, asked me to retrieve my Humpty Dumpty pieces and rearrange them into something new. I have been Broken Open. Have wandered in The Wilderness. Have been torn asunder in Shamanic Awakening. Have learned to Yield, when Life took the right of way.

Those were painful, heart shaping times, and I made it through. But I can't believe I'm back here again. What a terrible truth to know you will not be allowed to return to your former shell of self. That once again, I am busy collecting my pieces and letting Life pour something into me that I can't yet see.

I make it through my days with a pretty good front person who is going through the motions. Sometimes she even feels those motions and remembers what normal used to be. But it is nighttime where my containers dissolve, and I am left with all that feels dark and deep inside of myself. I can feel the inner kid sister who is in a state of shock, alternating between throwing a temper tantrum over how unfair this is and feeling paralyzed with disbelief. She feels like she needs hugs and cocoa and a better explanation than, "sometimes life just happens," for what has happened to her world.

I can also feel this angry, defensive, resentful part who wants to scream at people—*I'm not coming back!*—so horrifying and laborious is this internal journey. She feels like an adolescent howling at the world, pinging all over the place, and she can't emotionally regulate. She makes me feel anxious and panicky, and she wants to say shocking, wildly inappropriate things to people who complain about stuff that feels small and pale in her mind when contrasted with the scope of death.

Somewhere else inside is this woman who is trying to hold it all together and care for herself and her marriage and her parents and her practice and her life as best she can. She's got a good head on her shoulders and a million coping tools in her box, but she feels terribly worn down. Like an engine running out of steam that is going to one day stop on the tracks and never get going again.

And somewhere inside, there is a wise woman who tells me to just keep moving.

It would be easy to deny or dismiss their voices, but they all have something to say, all have a contribution to make in order to get me across this desert. That little girl mourns her brother and reminds me no amount of adult wisdom will ever replace the wisdom found in the heart of a child. Her love feels simple and uncomplicated. She loved him, because he was all she ever knew. And she misses him and tells me it is okay to miss with unvarnished ache.

That adolescent has so much to teach about what it is to be human, what it is to feel the unconstrained, full expression of who we are. She knows it is important to give voice to all the dreadful feelings inside of herself, that sometimes they can't help but spill out. That you have to feel them in order to bring healing to those wounds.

The woman holding it all together is telling me she needs rest and respite. Solitude and oasis. That she needs to lay the reigns down for awhile and not have to manage so terribly much. She's tired of over functioning in order to emotionally manage the spaces in her life, and she is knocking hard and fast at my door, telling me this coming year needs to be a year of change.

And that wise woman, her voice has been faint this week, but her presence is still there—she tells me that in order to make it across this barren space we are going to have to hold each other's hands, link up, and cross together. That the winds will be less likely to knock us down if we support each other. That we are stronger when we acknowledge and allow for the space of one another and focus on what unifies us instead of what divides.

It's not the first time she's given sage advice. I've learned through the lessons of my history that she always knows what is needed in any given situation. And so we link and try and make peace among ourselves. Try and make room for all parts and all expressions and all experiences of this awful tragedy. Try and see that all these feelings are rooted in, and a result of, love. Try and cross the horrible desert as a whole without leaving any part behind.

Maybe I'm not coming back, but I am coming through. However slow progress seems. Clutching the belief that something new will come from this. Somebody new. Some part of me born, emerging and learning to breathe, because of death.

We can't lose something precious to us, have something pass away, without something new eventually rising up. I can't see what that is tonight, can't connect with my sense that there are better things to come, but I have one teeny, tiny scrap of faith—so small right now, I'd almost think it didn't exist if I hadn't found from past experiences that a shred of faith, a whisper for *better*, a molecule of hope always remains, even in the most battered of hearts—and it is enough to keep me moving through the sands of this place.

The desert is long and harsh. But the link holds true.

36

Solitude becomes my oasis.
It becomes the still place
where I gather my energy
—waned by the excesses of grief—
back into myself.

And learn to hold it close.

37

TRICKSTERS

Rage. Anger. Hate. Bitterness. Resentment. Desolation. Isolation. Self-pity. Wretched Want.

*T*here may be some extraordinarily ugly emotions that come with grief. While I have learned that everybody handles these experiences differently, I have also learned that we truly do need to feel them in order to bring healing to ourselves. If we deny the monsters in our rooms they will only get bigger and louder, for they are simply trying to get our attention as they wait for our acknowledgment.

All of us owe it to ourselves and our own healing process to acknowledge the full spectrum of what we are feeling. There are some hard beasts to face inside of ourselves, and they will come out during a passage of grief, but they do not have to be ignored and hidden. In fact, the more we learn to listen to and make peace with our unpeaceable thoughts—by paying attention to what they have to say, honoring those feelings as valid, then choosing love anyways— the more we realize they are actually teachers in disguise, here to trick us into learning about humanity, forgiveness, and grace.

And that's the bottom line when it comes to monsters. If you sit with them long enough, find a way to look them square in the eye and face what seems so scary, you'll begin to find they are not so scary at all, but are instead tricksters that help us get in touch with the toughest, darkest, stuff of humanity, so we can learn to make a conscious choice about choosing love, choosing forgiveness, and choosing peace. Thereby becoming a willing participant in our own growth of the soul.

They trick us into exploring the dark, so we are better able to appreciate and embrace the grace of the light. After all, if we can learn to forgive and love over what feels dark inside of ourselves, how can we not then learn to begin to extend this same grace wherever we go?

To others. To our relationships. To our communities. To the world.

38

CHAOS AND LOVE

Denial.
Depression.
Bargaining.
Anger.
Numbness.
Emotional Outbursts.
Reentry troubles.
Adjustment.
Acceptance.

Stages of grief,
or so they say,
though I am left
holding all at once,
a disastrous mass
of jumbled lines
with a small
dot stating:
"Present Location."

There is nothing
linear about it,
and the best that
I can figure is
that grief is really
composed of just
two stages:
Chaos and Love.

Just like Life.
We are either
finding new creation

amidst the chaos
of change,
or remembering
what binds the
whole thing together
in the first place.

Love.

39

Every time I said:
It hurts, it hurts, it hurts.
Life answered:
Love heals, Love heals,
Love heals.

40

WASTELAND

People say that grief is like the ocean, and it is in many ways. Coming and going like the tide, as it nips at your toes and reminds you of its presence. Washing you into its powerful waves, churning you upside down until you don't know which way is which. Washing you into its massive embrace, each shifting moment a different shade of sea.

*Y*es, grief can be like the ocean, but I have found the heart of grief to be more the dry, barren wasteland. Endless in view. Oases few. The blast of the relentless sun unforgiving in nature.

Grief eviscerates. Makes you feel like you are crawling, trying to scratch your way through the haze of parched pain. Grabbing for anything that might quench your unquenchable thirst.

The wasteland is where you come face to face with the heart of your pain. The wasteland is where you will feel destroyed and erased. The wasteland is where you fall off the edges of yourself, fall off the edges of reality as you knew it. The wasteland is where you find out what you're made of when life knocks you to the ground, and you are forced to go on all fours.

I know it may seem like you will never emerge, will never find your feet again, will be forever crawling, but *my dear friend*, I can tell you from one who has had many a crawl herself, there are gifts on the ground that we do not always see from the height of the sky. Gifts of sand and stone and roots, which remind us we are being held up by the power of the earth and are supported by more than just ourselves in this space. Gifts of cooling, underground water reserves when we learn how to dig deep.

Gifts of a humble heart and tired spirit and hurting mind that leave us desperately seeking—and therefore more likely to *see*—the mercy that is running through the marrow of these days. Gifts of strength that come when we look back, see the ground we've passed, and realize: this is horrible and brutal and hard, but I made it this far and see how strong I've become.

Because. I. Am. Still. Going.

41

HOUSE OF HEALING

If not love, then fear. And goodness knows there's enough fear in the world already. So I choose love.

A few weeks back, I wrote about my future self helping pull me through the longevity of sadness that has composed my recent days. This week, I am trying to allow my past self to soothe and inspire. I've spent my morning reading old postings on my blog, studying the words of my younger self, taking their messages into me, and using their medicine of love as a balm for my ravaged heart.

As I read my words of days gone by, I see a girl who has hope and joy. I see a girl who made some very brave choices in her life that caused her soul to grow in leaps and bounds. I see a girl who went through more heartaches and betrayals than she cares to count. Who found out the hard way that those who engage with the world with the whole of their heart will often end up getting hurt in the game of love. Who learned that love should never be a game to begin with, because people should not play the heart strings of others to satisfy their own songs of self.

I see a girl who saw some very ugly things in life, including inside herself, and decided to choose love anyway. For the world. For others. Most of all for herself. I see wisdom and experience arise where naiveté and inexperience once lay. I see the wounded healer learn how to heal her wounds, so she can better heal others. I see a girl who learns the true meaning of self-love, and, as she is writing her own love story of self, unexpectedly falls in love. I see both their love stories, hers and his, intertwine into a story of becoming and coming home.

Then I see 2016 arrive, and I see the beginning of this story of terrible tragedy that has haunted my heart ever since. I don't know how it will end; I'm still writing it as I go.

I miss you, somebody told me the other day. *Yeah, I get it, I miss me too*, I thought. I miss that girl who wrote those stories, the one who used to smile and laugh so easily and give of her generous heart so consistently and openly. I miss that girl who had the luxury of living in a world where her brother is alive, a world where she isn't being forced to roll up her sleeves and confront the ugly truths of grief and death, along with a maelstrom of stress that hit from other directions this season, leaving her shaking her head at the timing of life.

I've been in dark nights of the soul before, and I find myself in one again, as I wonder what I'm supposed to learn from all this. Currently, my compass feels broken, and I seem to have exceeded my abilities to navigate the dark. I know I have to do my own work; nobody else can do it for me. I am the only one who can find the answers I need for the lessons of my soul, and, right now, the only thing I know to do is to find my answers through the act of living the questions.

At present, I am in the thick of the chaos, but the worst and the best part of the process is that I already know the questions will somehow be answered by Love. For every good and true thing I have found in this life, everything I have ever overcome, everything I have worked so hard to become, is all sealed together with Love. Even if I can't quite see its picture right now.

I have some temporary walls up that don't usually exist. Spaces erected to create an incubator of protection during this grief state that, I keep unfortunately learning, can't be rushed through. So I have built a house of healing inside of myself to care for my angry ego, my tired body, and my wounded heart. Maybe I look like an isolationist state, but it's not forever, just for now. And I assume that when the time is right I will simply knock them down. I already know I won't need the walls where I'm going: Love has no walls.

My past self already learned how to live this truth beautifully. So today I will draw on her wisdom and close with words she wrote two years ago. They have such a sense of eerie resonance, I can't help but think that just as my future self waits before, helping pull me at this time, my younger self is busy pushing me from the past, having written the very words she knew I would need to hear today

74

to remember what it's all about and to keep giving myself permission
to be what I need.

There may come a day where you change the rules.
There may come a day where you say not that,
but this is what I need.
There may come a day where your spirit beckons so strong
you shudder in assent with the call of truth, an unwitting participant
in your own higher plan for you.
And when this day comes you must be prepared to take your strong
stout warrior heart
and remake the rules in accordance with your truth of soul.
Then bravely cast your fate into the wind to fall where you may,
to fall where life calls,
to fall where Love needs you to go.

42

And sometimes help arrives softly.
In small flakes that cover the dirtiness of the season
and bring thoughts of white light and snow angels
and how life can sanctify anything
—even the gritty, dusty, devastation of grief—
with a covering of new bright.

It's called grace.

Life is full of it.

43

FIGHT

I can feel her in my corner.
She's been standing there
watching the knockout.

All knowing, she knows that
animals have an instinct to
curl into a hole after they've
been hurt, and she knows
humans have both instinct
and choice.

Get up! she says.
You're going to have to choose
to fight. It's going to hurt,
all good things do.

Don't do it because others
think you should.
Don't do it because your
brother would want you to.
Don't do it because people
are counting on you.

Those things are not enough.
You're going to have to do it for you.
Only you can decide you're worth it.
But trust me you are, so get up.

Fight.

44

HERO

It is remarkable how much can change in the span of a week. These last few months are some of the worst months I have lived. In addition to the senseless loss of my brother, life has churned up the waters with so much stress and turmoil, I've carried a heaviness of spirit I've struggled to bear.

I have been waiting for some sort of bailout from life. Some magic solution to fix all the day to day stuff that is clogging up my arteries of peace. The ghost of my brother to show up and give me a recitation on the secrets of life and somehow provide me with enough information that I have a spiritual *aha!* moment, helping me make sense of everything. The friend who just shows up on the doorstep with hot soup and a listening ear and the perfect words of comfort that somehow make it all right again.

A winning lottery ticket. A super power. A miracle. Something, anything, to pull me out of the choppy seas in which I've been drowning.

I never imagined that something would be me.

It started last Sunday when I began to read old posts on my blog. They made me remember where I came from, and I found so much strength and truth and heart in the words that they reminded me of something I almost forgot: my ability to rescue myself. They reminded me of all the other times I felt I was drowning in life's choppy seas, how I couldn't find my way out, and how I bravely weathered every storm, until I eventually found myself standing on new shore.

They reminded me of that brave girl who blindly leapt off the precipice of faith each time she felt life was guiding her there, leaving the secure certitude of land for the amorphous possibility of air. They reminded me that when I responded in faith, life never let me fall. Not once. Even when I couldn't see the way.

Through my own words, I discovered a one woman cheer squad shouting through her megaphone about love, authenticity, self-discovery, and things that bring us true sustenance. She knows these things, because she has lived and integrated their lessons into her life, and who she is inside matches how she acts and behaves in life. She is in alignment with her highest truths and not afraid to live them.

She is my higher self, and if it is possible for our higher self to reach down and pull us out of the ocean when we most badly need an assist, then she arrived just in time with a smile on her face and a strong, capable hand that yanked me out of the abyss and deposited me on a shore I've never seen before. It's uncharted territory whose scope I am still learning, I just know there is a lot of possibility here.

This is the first time in almost 3 months, where instead of curling up into the fist of life or swimming for all I'm worth in those hideous seas of grief, that I feel myself slowly standing up, curling my own fist and preparing to fight for what is mine: my life. It doesn't matter how unfair it is that Brent died. It doesn't matter that I can't wrap my mind around how somebody can just fall down and be gone; why tragedy and struggle hit some people so hard, while others appear to go relatively unscathed.

It doesn't matter that life has broken me open before, and here I am again, lost in the dark as I search for my pieces. None of that matters when it comes down to the bigger question: how will you answer the call of your own life?

My words this past weekend re-reminded me that nobody is going to do the work for me. If I want beauty, if I want truth, if I want happiness, if I want love, if I want to live my truths, if I want a full life, then I am going to have to fight for myself. Even if I have to walk through miles of darkness to do so. So I dug a little deeper than I thought was possible. I reached a little higher than I thought I could. I found some untapped reservoir hiding inside of me that I didn't know existed, and I uncurled those fists and went to work.

And I wrote a book.

I collected every piece of writing from back in that time period. I ordered them with all sorts of creative flair. I edited and reedited and am still editing. I put pages together of heart and sweat and tears, which I once spilled trying to find my way through darkness. I wrote about finding light, and courage, and spirit through pages of poetry, quotes, and prose.

As I put the whole thing together, I had the odd sense that if not for this exact set of circumstances and my own furious attempts to grab onto something substantial that I could hang onto in the hopelessness of this space, I wouldn't have found what I needed to write this book. My desperation has become my mother of reinvention.

I've been saying I want to write books for years, yet I cut myself off at the knees every time I tried by talking myself out of the work, telling myself it wasn't good enough, and never making it past the first page. But now, because of Brent, I have become fearless and terribly aware of how incredibly short life can be. This loss is giving me the courage to live bigger and braver, to realize that at some point I have to stop playing small and own my own sense of being enough.

So I go to work. Spend the weekend writing. Begin to see a tangible vision take shape before me, which only seemed a vague dream weeks back.

Now, I find myself with a manuscript on my computer that tells a story of bravery, love, and being human. My words of yesterday have reached into an inner void and begun to heal something that feels broken. I don't know if I can say exactly what, I just know something that was missing is being born again. And I know that there is no way I am going to let down that brave girl of my yesterdays who worked so hard to make herself into this big, bright, beautiful person.

She is a believer. And she made me believe in something again. Fervently. To never give up on ourselves. To never stay in complacency if Life is calling us towards something more. To find the faith to leap off the cliff, even if there is no safety net. That true love and happiness and change are all inside jobs, which we cannot outsource.

That the best hero we can have in our life is our self.

45

POSSIBILITIES

There were moments of aching clarity after my brother's death where I realized I would give anything to go back to how things were before and have a normal "bad day."

That I would give anything for him to be here and be in a bad mood, have a sibling spat, have normal family concerns. That I would give anything not to have to process the loss of all the places he will never go, all the things he will never do, and all the future memories we will never make.

That I would give anything for things to be normal, because even on the worst of days, normal still included him in the picture instead of the hole that his presence once filled.

It is a privilege: Life. And we don't always see or appreciate that until a life is gone, and we realize that as long as we are HERE—in this time and space—possibilities for more and for better exist. Part of grief work is learning to come face to face with that lack of possibility once somebody has passed on and learning to come to terms with the timeline they lived out on this earth.

Learning to come to terms with Brent no longer having possibilities is an ongoing work in progress. Trying to make peace with the serrated, ripped ending of his story feels like trying to make peace with the impossible. But I work at it anyways, let the tender ravages of my heart be a soapstone that gently exfoliates the roughest parts of the story and the extinguishing of possibility.

And somewhere in the middle of this work, I have become increasingly aware that the only way I can honor what had come to pass—to live in such a way as to realize how brief a spark our time can be—is to fully embrace and embody the only thing I can control:

The light of my own possibility.

46

NEW SHELL

I wonder when
people look at me
if they see I am just
an old shell.

With fire in my eyes
and fury in my fingers
to keep my
seeds warm.

There is a new world
growing in my soul,
soon it will crack
me open—

I'm anxious to see
what I'll become.

47

ILLUMINATION

We think that enlightenment—moving towards a fuller sense of clarity, truth, and illumination in our lives—is a peaceful, zen laden path.

$\mathcal{B}$ut I have found that this simply isn't true at all, and any time we turn the lights on in a previously dark and unexplored place, we are going to become aware of all the cobwebs, clutter and dust that has collected and will need to spend some time cleaning before that space feels clear.

On the first day of the new year, I declared 2016 the Year of Illumination. I wanted to set my intention that this year be one of greater truth, integrity, and honesty for my life. And it has been… just not in the way I expected. As it turns out, death is the greatest illuminator of all, taking you to your core, making you sit with what is most real, turning the lights on in the rooms of your life, exposing all that is crowding those spaces, inviting you to declutter.

This is hard work. Unglamorous. Sometimes miserable. We cannot step into a fuller awareness of our lives and our self without the painful process of examining and sorting through our emotional, spiritual, and relational spaces. I often had the sense of being squeezed and stretched this past season, like life was tugging at both ends of something invisible, but tangible, inside. Pulling and siphoning, clearing and cleaning, trying to make space for something new.

There was nothing zen about it. But there was something honest: my unvarnished truth. A greater sense of purpose, insight, and awareness of my place in the pattern and the direction I want to continue to shape my life.

Grief will shine a light into every corner of us if we let it, and there is much we stand to gain when we allow the light to stay on. A deepening relationship with Life and Ourselves, which helps us live with greater intent, meaning, and authenticity. A deepening relationship with Spirit, which holds the potential to help us step more fully into the truth of who we are. A deepening relationship with Love, which holds the key to changing the shape and scope of our hearts.

Humanity is messy, Spirit divine, and we are lucky enough to be graced with both. And it will take both—plumbing the depths of our recesses and bringing whatever we find out into the light so we can live an examined life AND finding perspective and relationship with Life that extends and embraces something beyond just ourselves—if we want to find the courage to live a life of illumination.

48

THE WORKBENCH

There are so many flowers I can't stop taking pictures. Reds and pinks and bright lavenders punctuate the hundred shades of green found among all the leaves and fronds. I'm in Oregon right now, visiting family, enjoying time off, hungering for change.

*N*ot the kind of change found externally, more like the kind of change found internally that makes me want to change the channel on myself and fast forward to a different version who hasn't quite finished spinning herself out. The writer in me knows that any good manuscript takes patience and labor and careful crafting before a finished product spins itself out. The human in me feels tired of sitting at her workbench, impatient with life, weary of the emotional consequences of loss.

I have been working on radical gratitude during this trip. Finding appreciation in the colors and new scenery and change of pace. Finding appreciation for how far I've come these past few months and how much I've learned about love and hope and heart. Finding appreciation for the possibility of change and the knowledge that no season lasts forever.

Be in this moment, I keep telling myself. *No matter if it's not your endgame, and you still feel you are shedding the sticky layers of grief's cocoon. Just be in this moment.*

Yesterday was the 4-month mark of my brother's passing, and I find it both poetic, uncanny, and lovely that I was able to spend the day with his best friend. Jon lives in Washington, just a short drive away, and we while away the afternoon remembering, having moments of happiness and sadness, as we trade stories of the Brent we knew. He, like me, is a member of the very small club of people who is profoundly impacted by this death.

We already share the same unspoken language of loss; conversation comes easy. His girlfriend, Kristina, knew my brother too, and they both share anecdotes of Brent's antics and humor that left everyone in stitches, while my husband and I learn about this outrageous, rock star, huge personality that emerged in their tight knit friendship.

It is a gift to have someone give you new stories about a loved one you've lost. It's like creating new memories posthumously, those memories becoming infinitely precious, because you've lost the opportunity to create new ones. I gather these bits and pieces of remembrance like rare gemstones, tiny sparkling diamonds that give me new facets on who Brent was as a friend.

Last night, I thought about those gifts and reflected that a couple months back, I was in such a dark and lonely space of loss that I wrote about wishing I had a time machine to zip me six months ahead, so the worst of the heaviness of loss would be behind me. Some days I still wish for that time machine; though the sun is getting brighter in the season, I can still feel great, great waves of sadness roiling around inside of me, and I find them difficult to carry.

But I also know that if I zipped ahead, I wouldn't have been present yesterday and have new memories to treasure. I wouldn't be here in Salem enjoying the play of the breeze and snapping pictures of all that is blue, lush, and green, as I create more new memories with my husband's huge hearted mother and crowd of colorful siblings. I wouldn't have run through gorgeous, mile-high stretches of old pine and had an incredible flash of inspiration for a book on grief, which is going to be my next writing project. I wouldn't be writing the words I am now. And I wouldn't be sitting here on this workbench, sometimes doing my own chiseling and sometimes allowing life to chisel me, as some new beauty inside of myself continues to be fine tuned and worked out.

Be in this moment. Sometimes that is the best we can do when life has brought us to a space of transition. Breathe and allow space for what is. Insist on finding gratitude for any and every little thing we possibly can. Let life's winds sweep through us, rustling change on our leaves, as we give ourselves over to the making.

49

RELENTLESS GRATITUDE

Gratitude
is as elusive
as the breeze…
one moment here
next moment gone—

if you sit back
and wait
for it to make
its way
to you.

Instead you
must learn to
pursue it
relentlessly
incessantly
tenaciously,
working hard
to hold it in
your grasp.

It is just
that hard
and that easy
to find joy
in this world:

Refuse to give
up on finding
what is good,

what is sacred,
what is lovely,
and you'll begin
to see—

All of it is
a grace.
And worthy
of our thanks.

50

THE LAST SUPPER

There are still days when I hurt for my brother so much my insides pain. It's inescapable. Following me wherever I go, no matter how hard I try to get away.

Following me to Oregon and up to its coast, melding with ocean and sky and forest and bliss, until I can't tell where I joy and where I ache. Following me back to the familiar thrum of life in Anchorage, reminding me that life as I knew it is no longer. Following me as I try to pick up some of my old threads.

Following me when I show up for a friend's birthday dinner, one of the first social functions I've attended in months. I'd like to feel normal, be just one of the girls, except I walk into the restaurant and am absolutely flooded by the realization that this is the place I last saw my brother. Christmas Eve: his red wine and filet mignon, my white wine and veggie pad thai, I almost took a picture of us that night, remembered he hated pictures, stilled my hand instead.

Regrets. I'd give much for one last picture.

I try and put a smile on my face and fake the night and laughter and cupcakes. Try and be present as I scream in my head, cry in the bathroom, turn and stare at the table where we had our last supper. I want to freeze time and see if I can recapture my memory of that night, go sit with him one last time to take in his full... even as I think about how unfair life can be and how unavoidable is the grief that comes when somebody who was rooted so close to you is suddenly uprooted, and you're left to cope with the destructive remains of deforestation.

Nothing but wide open spaces, miles of rootless tears, and acres of unanswered questions on how to rebuild and regrow. I understand why people go crazy after loss and just can't seem to get it back together. I understand why people who love too fast and too hard find themselves broken in grief and never find their missing pieces. I understand why people feel forced to reinvent themselves elsewhere and search for new pieces to plug in the holes they can no longer fill; there are some breaks that can't be sealed back up. Maybe they aren't meant to.

Society says, *Get over it, move on, your pain is uncomfortable.*

I say, *I hurt. I can't. A piece of my heart died with my brother, I'm desperately trying to regrow.*

I have no answers for any of this at present. I feel like I'm moving forward only to find myself back. I find new ground only to feel it slip out from under my feet. I thought it would be better by now, but nobody told me it would look like this and still anguish so hard after 4 and a half months. I'm trying to practice radical self-compassion, turn my back on any voice that judges and misunderstands grief. Trying to let myself continue to feel what I feel as long as I need to feel.

Trying to remember: there are some breaks we are not meant to get over, some holes not meant to be filled. Life isn't meant to be cohesive, just transformative. We the unwitting passengers, bound up in its days.

51

FORGOTTEN FLOWERS

I'd wring it out of me
if I could, this sadness.

Like a sponge, I'd squeeze myself
dry over the land
and water the forgotten flowers
with my sorrow.

I'd cast my woes into the belly
of the ocean,
far, far, far from me…
after all, what's a few more
drops in the sea?

I've asked the thirsty land
to take it from me
many times, but she gently tells me
it's mine to carry.

That sorrow softens
hard angles and plains, taking
what's harsh in the heart
and bringing it light.

That grace is found
when we acknowledge our pain,
yet choose to seek joy
despite.

52

Take courage my dear heart,
for time will eventually help
mend your wounds.

And I promise
you will once again
find your way.

53

GET OVER IT

You don't have to get over it.

You don't have to get over it 6 months from now. You don't have to get over it 6 years from now. You don't have to get over it 60 years from now. In fact, there may always be a small part of you frozen in the thick of grief. Curled up by the tomb of the loss where you laid a piece of you to rest the day you lost *them*. Kneeling in honor for that which fell too soon.

You do not have to get over it. But you do have to keep getting on. Trying to put one foot in front of the other. Trying to do life. Trying to move through and see if you can find new life on the other side. You owe it to yourself; you owe it to your grief, which reminds you how fiercely you loved; you owe it to your massive heart who is busy crawling forward, struggling to try. To move. To search for all that is good and true and bright.

To find the light amidst the pain.

In the hopes that someday, whenever that day may be, you find that while you were busy watering the land with grief, life grew roses around the place where your loss resides. Giving you hope and a reminder that despite the pain that marks that place, life will find a way to keep growing. Easing the pain. Reminding you profound good happens too.

Covering what aches with the only balm that will soothe the pain. Love.

54

WHY NOT

These days I am learning
when to allow descent
into the awful abyss,
to find life's glorious diamonds
amongst the blackest black

And when to extend
a helping hand to myself,
so I can rise above the clouds
and see things through
a lens of light.

These days I am learning
how to sit in discomfort
and feel my skin stretch

— — —

into a new skin of self.

These days I am learning
that *why not?*
is a far better response
than *why?*
and a very good answer
if the question is:

The reasons you think you can't.

These days I am learning
that far worse than feeling
the pain of change,
is living with the pain of never
truly knowing yourself.

55

I REMEMBER

Other people are going to forget what feels so immediate to you as time goes on. And that can be hard.

I am grieving, I'm in pain, my insides have been ripped to shreds, you'll think when they ask you how you're doing. And though to you it feels like it was just yesterday, to them weeks or months or maybe even years have spun out, and so many things have continued to happen, they may not remember what feels like such a fresh imprint on your heart.

We don't have traditions in our society that mark those who go through grief. We don't wear a special ribbon or dress in black for months or get to take a year off life to properly see ourselves through all the tasks of loss. Instead, life pauses in those brief instances when if first happens and space is created for the memorial and immediate grief, but then, ready or not, we are expected to get on about the business of living again.

The problem for many of us is that we are not ready to get on in the land of the living, as we still have a foot firmly planted in the land of the dying.

It is in our nature to want to seek to understand and make sense of the mysteries in this place, and when somebody leaves us, I believe a part of us dies with them. It is the part of ourselves who knew them and cherished them and thought they'd still be here. It is the person we were before they passed and the person who didn't expect things to turn out like this. It is our sense of a physical day to day relationship, as we go to pick up the phone or send a text or give a hug and realize over and over, they are no longer here.

I spend my winter trying to understand the nature of death. *What does it mean, where did he go, can I sense him out there, how can somebody just up and die so suddenly like that?* I keep wanting to reach through the void, snatch him back, put him where he belongs in our family, put everything back in its place again.

I am left with nothing but questions and irresolution and holes in a timeline that make no sense to me. I stare out the window at the dead branches on the trees, go for quiet walks in the woods on the icy winter trails, wonder at how so much death comes to pass in this place, yet the world still finds a way to keep giving birth to new life over and over and over again.

What is it all about? Why are we here? What does it all mean? These aren't new questions for me, but they are questions from a different angle filtered through the lens of loss, and as such they become very different questions than I've wondered before, and it takes time for me to fill in the gaps and start to create a timeline that makes some semblance of reason in my own mind.

In my alone hours, I talk to the sky and the clouds and the sun constantly. I curl up against a tree in those quiet walks I take and, even in winter, let the heartbeat of the land support me. I isolate and insulate and try and take all the space I need to honor my profound sense of loss, even though Life is carrying on around me and people are starting to wonder if I'm okay.

I'm not okay though. And I realize that many people, unacquainted with this kind of loss, are ill advised to tell me what to do at this point, so I start making up my own rituals and give myself permission to not be okay.

I travel to rural Canada all by myself on a spiritual pilgrimage that takes me to a Full Moon Ceremony in a Native American lodge, where I learn how water is life, how it is constantly cleansing us, how we can offer our problems up to Grandmother Moon and find release. I sit in the sharing circle that night trying to speak of why I am there, why this woman from Alaska has traveled thousands of miles to Manitoba to come sit in this space of woman's ceremony.

I try to share about the loss of my brother, how sometimes we have to travel far outside the lines of ourselves in order to find what we're seeking within. Try to tell them the truth of why I have come, but my lip is quivering so hard and my voice is close to hyperventilation as big salty tears trickle down my face, and my thin veneer of control is preciously close to breaking.

I can feel she is right at the surface that night—the little girl inside of me shouting, shouting, shouting—*It's not fair, it's not fair, it's not fair!* She doesn't understand why her brother had to die, doesn't understand all these big spiritual ideas about Life and Love and The Universe. Nor does she care. She is content to lay on the floor kicking and screaming for all she is worth. Nobody asked her if it was okay to take her brother away. She didn't even get to say goodbye, and she has a lot to say about it.

This is the weekend I learn: you don't leave grief behind you just because you travel thousands of miles away. That no amount of healing ceremonies, or time spent in prayer and contemplation, or time spent in utter solitude and retreat manages to shift my sense that I have been slowly climbing up a mountain while dragging a bag of rocks the equivalent of my brother's weight. That only time and love are going to bring any sort of solace to this particular wound.

However, I do feel profound Grace that weekend. Connection. Higher Power. Source. The Force. My spiritual pilgrimage is not in vain, and I can feel Love supporting me, though I still have my heavy mass of grief. And this is when I truly experience and realize: nobody can carry this for me. Nobody can dive into my internal world and take my loss away. I am the only one who can carry this. Nobody else can do my work or is going to feel the loss of what it meant to be Brent's sister.

This is the cost of loving my brother. How could anybody else possibly pay a sister's price?

And that takes me back to the beginning words I wrote: *Other people are going to forget what feels so immediate to you as time goes on. And that can be hard.*

It's not their fault though. Truly it isn't. Our losses are our own to carry, our grief creating unique breaks and changes and patterns inside each of us that we must learn to integrate into the whole of who we are. And while we can absolutely look to our relationships to make things lighter for one another along the journey—offering support and kind words and practical aspects of help—the emotional, mental, physical, and spiritual work of grief is our own to resolve.

As winter begins to thaw and spring gently begins to wake back up, I work hard at nurturing that little girl who is crying over her brother. I work hard at showing up for myself, being my own wise woman, and giving myself permission to be and do and feel whatever

I need in these moments. I slowly begin to take one foot outside the space of death and remember what it is to plant both feet in the space of life.

I work hard to release any resentment or bitterness or lack of forgiveness I feel towards people who didn't know how to support me through my grief, who haven't experienced it themselves, who didn't know the right thing to say to me, so they said nothing at all. I work hard at finding compassion for a society who—at least the vast majority—is so uncomfortable with the idea of death, grief, and loss that they choose denial, avoidance, and distraction over learning to feel what is most real.

I work hard at having compassion for all people who have suffered loss, and I dedicate the wounds I feel to anyone who has ever suffered silently; I give my wounds purpose, offering them up to life as restitution for those whose losses have never been given voice. I work hard at having compassion for myself, for recognizing my fragility and vulnerability, as I am but a shell of my old self.

There is a new me slowly beginning to rise up like the spring buds on the trees, but not quite ready to leave this space of hibernation and open up. I learn to *be* in this uncomfortable space of transformation. I learn that the only zen I find in the chaos is an unwavering commitment to loving all parts of myself during this sorrowful, strange, sad season. I learn to grow while standing still and trust my blooms to open when it is time.

I realize, as winter melts to spring and slowly begins to seep into summer, that I am doing it, I am carrying it. I have made it up much of that mountain with the weight of my brother attached to my ankles, have grown strong from having to sit and face this horrible reality of loss, have learned new ways of entreating with life that help me to journey on. And it begins to matter less that other people seem to have forgotten—I welcome but no longer seek their support and validation—I remember, I always will. And in the process, I have become an extremely strong woman.

I have lived what it means to carry him wherever I go.

56

OPEN AT THE CLOSE

Our times march on
our stories go
and life shifts underneath,
we breathe in love
we exhale loss—
and open at the close.

We learn to hurt
then learn to reach
then learn the grace of grief,
our hearts contract
then learn to grow—
hearts open with a close.

You went away
you left so soon
your light abruptly spent,
but death begins
your journey forth—
you opened at your close.

We cannot choose
our breaks in life
the things that rearrange,
but we can choose
to look for light—
and open when we close.

Go on take heed
when sorrows come

and let tears drench your face,
for water cleans

and clears new space—
life opens with a close.

So carry on
and love what's gone
your life forever changed,
but let your heart
stay soft to mold—
love opens at the close.

Summer

GRIEF'S RELIEF

My heart grows where my sorrow goes,
grief's pain reveals the light.

57

*Horrible things can come
from something that seems beautiful,
and beautiful things can come from something
that seems horrible.*

Who's to say what's better?

58

SEND

It is remarkable how scary it can be to click the word "send."

I sent an email this morning to a potential publisher inquiring if they are taking submissions, and that small simple act has taken me almost a month to do. I keep using the excuse that I am still cleaning up my poetry manuscript, but the truth is I've been stalling, having doubts about my own work and fears about putting myself out there on a larger level. Fears about the consequences of the unknown juggernaut of change we create in our lives when we dare to move in a new direction.

Pretty much the same doubts that have a tendency to hold any of us back when we defend our fears and constraints and limitations instead of arguing in favor of the unfathomable.

I am learning that moving forward doesn't always look the way you thought it would. You don't necessarily get back on track, you just find a way to keep stepping. The last few weeks have arranged themselves into an absurd pattern of 2 steps forward, 4 steps back, 10 steps forward, 5 steps back, 3 steps to the side, 7 steps in a circle… toss in a few electric slides, and I've been doing a bizarre line dance with no rhyme or reason, and I can no longer keep track of where I'm standing.

I am also learning to stop tracking my movement by trying to number my steps, and instead track my movement by my experience— *Am I growing? Am I learning new things? Am I discovering new emotional states? Am I increasing in love?* As opposed to nonsensical, random quantification—*Do I cry less? Do I have more good days than bad? Is my grief lessening? Do I seem normal yet?*

I can't answer the latter: sometimes it's a *yes*, sometimes *no*. But I can answer the former with a definitive, *Yes I am*, that reminds me the evolution of the heart cannot be measured by numbers or achievements or successes, instead, it reveals its process through the sincerity of love we bring to the world.

I now know that like love and snowflakes and people, there are no two griefs alike. You could ask any of us who have gone through shocking, forever changes you, horrible kinds of losses to write a book on our experience, and every manuscript would be different. Of course we would see familiar themes, truths, and shared experiences among the writings, but the nuances of emotion, the meaning derived, the ways we found to make it through—each scribble would have its own unique fingerprint, its own unique contribution to the whole.

So it is with grief and so it is with us. No two experiences alike. No two processes alike. No two journeys alike. We each have our own unique contribution to the whole.

This past season, I have been working on learning to accept my personal experiences as valid and true and part of my whole without the need for others to approve, validate, or make sense of them for me. There is so much of the crazy, nonsensical, steps to the dance of losing my brother that will never figure, but the things I have learned along the way are beginning to turn into something more than just a few forward steps here and a few backwards steps there.

Instead, they are transforming into a different vision for life than the one I would have imagined a year ago. It's beautiful and scary and doubt filled and will require loads of courage and faith, but I see changes coming down the pike that feel warm to my soul, despite their daunting face, and I know ultimately that anything that feels warm to your soul is always a good thing.

In the meantime, change begins with that single step in a new direction. Sometimes it means you wander off the path for a bit. Let the steps of nonsensical faith in the unfathomable lead you somewhere else. Walk away from that same old mountain you've been climbing, because though there is nothing wrong with that particular mountain and there were many beautiful lessons once found there, you have come to a place in your journey where it has nothing new to teach you.

Rather, you find yourself going into the woods for awhile to a place you've never been before. You lean against a tree, think about its cycles of change, give yourself permission to change, too. You notice how big the sky is and how limitless the possibilities. You let Life support you, and you find the courage to press "send."

59

There may not always be
happy endings,
but there are new stories to write.

Life is meant to be lived
forwards, not back.

60

SHINE

There are going to be days where the sun shines a little bit brighter. If you're not there yet, I promise you they will come. There will be days where the grief isn't as potent, and the light slips its way through the clouds and brings you warm grace.

*A*nd when those days come, let them. You have nothing to feel guilty about for feeling good. The grief is there, it isn't going anywhere, feeling good doesn't mean you're not grieving. It just means you are beginning to open to life again. Beginning to take in the joys and the goods that will slowly begin to impress themselves upon your psyche, reminding you there is still life out there waiting to be lived.

Everything has a season, even grief, and it will make itself known in its own time on its own accord. So on those days where the clouds part and the winds stir and the light comes in? Let it shine. Bask in it. Take it into you like medicinal balm, let it warm your spirits and help restore you to life.

Then know you've been given the medicine of grace.

61

FIFTY-TWO

Fifty-two. The number of weeks I have left in Alaska. Well, give or take a few since life can sometimes have its own timetable, but approximately one year from today we will be pulling up stakes and moving on across the waters to Kauai.

I drove to work this week thinking of the number 52 in my mind. That if things do fall out the way we've projected, the end of May will be when I formally close my practice, and we will go jump on a plane with a couple of dogs and a temperamental calico cat—an image that has me shaking my head when I think about all the hoops needed to jump through to make that happen.

Moving is hard enough, but moving to an island feels extra challenging. It's huge massive change, so much so that it's hard to wrap my head around the amount of letting go, and goodbyes, and leave takings that are going to take place in the next year. Let alone the details of selling a house and moving our stuff and closing a long term practice.

And all the unknowns! What we will do when we get there, where will we live, how will we live? I can only imagine how sparse things might be for awhile, where luxuries like travel and going out to eat and buying that new pair of shoes will not likely be possible until we get our feet underneath us.

But I'm counting on the beauty of the place, and the fact that I can go sit on a beach whenever I like, to make up for any lack and help me see there are greater things than money that constitute lack. Like not listening to the call of your soul, forcibly smothering your courage, turning down your own volume of voice that urges you to *go*.

It can be daunting. All the things that can feel like roadblocks if we let them, but they're really not. They are difficulties, variables, challenges. Not impossibilities. At one point in time, Kauai felt like an impossibility, but I am finding that if I just allow myself to look at it differently, see things from the angle of "can" instead of "can't," that it isn't an impossibility after all. Just a process of figuring out how to navigate an obstacle course.

Last June I wrote a piece called "Speed Bumps." It used the literal and metaphorical idea of the speed bumps around the town of Anchorage to take a trip down memory line and reflect on different points in my history where a particular speed bump got in my way, tripped me up, slowed me down, and disrupted my flow.

It is the story about my own growth and evolution in this town which ends with my deep yearning that, despite all the gifts of growth that have come from life in Anchorage, someday I will live someplace where there are not so many speed bumps. Not so many visceral reminders of my past popping up all over the place, making me pause and remember things I've laid to rest. One can only reinvent themselves so many times over in the same space before they hunger for a new place to plant roots and grow.

Then Brent happened, and all of Anchorage has become a giant speed bump, even with my best efforts to find the beauty and good in each day. This has been home for over 30 years, housing the 4 members of my core family all that time; Dad, Mom, Brent, and I; we grew up here; laid deep roots. And now there are 3, and it's all been uprooted, and I no longer want to live in the place that played host to so much loss.

And so I find myself in a new place of possibility, ready to leave the familiarity of life in Alaska. Life After Brent has pushed me to go. Stripped me of who and what isn't real in my life. Challenged me to consider what I am doing with my time, if I am living the life I want to live. Yanked me from the ease of shadows on the wall of the cave— representing certainty, security, and comfort—and forced me out into the release of the sun, who tells me I need to find new ways to let the sun shine brighter in my life.

I'm choosing to interpret this literally by moving to a place where you can depend on the sun shining bright. A place where I don't ever have to be bone achingly, smothered in darkness, cold again.

There is a strange acceptance found when we begin to let go. An odd peace that casts a soft glow and sense of nostalgia over everything. Though it's still a year out, I find myself saying goodbye to people and places and old spaces in preparation for the change. Find myself loosening the angles and grooves in the old shapes I once fit; I no longer have to squeeze myself into those molds. Find myself letting the threads of how life was supposed to look unravel. Find the beauty in the becoming found in life's undoings.

Brent was forced becoming. Forced change. Forced loss. I had no warning, no do overs, no chance to say goodbye, and that has taught me many radical lessons on acceptance, letting go, making peace with imperfect endings, and finding gratitude for what was and what is. We are not promised tomorrow, best to find peace in today, and so I find myself in the right heart space for change.

Besides, unlike with Brent, I have the opportunity to say goodbye to Anchorage. To tie up what I can. To loosen what needs to be loosened. To say anything that lays unspoken, though I have learned we always have an opportunity to say those words; just because something has already passed doesn't mean you can't speak the words you need to say into life anyway and trust they'll travel to wherever they need to go.

To allow my heart to find and feel whatever it needs in the amount of time left. Time that is precious and finite, filled with sorrow and joy, a closing of the old to create an opening for the new. Time that I suspect, will pass all too slowly and all too swiftly.

Fifty-two weeks.

62

THE GIFT

I have never known
such profound
sorrow
for the still of grief,
or such exquisite
beauty
for the grace of life.

And I keep finding
where one ends
the other begins.

It is a gift:
this breath of time.
One that begs no payment
other than we do
our best to learn to love
and try to
live it well.

63

FOREVER 39

Yesterday would have been my brother's 40ᵗʰ birthday. I don't know exactly how I feel about that except to say that yesterday I was spacy all day long— my thoughts closer to the stars than the earth—and my heart kept its own rhythm, rising and falling with the sorrows of the sea.

I wonder sometimes as I walk around and watch other people do life if they know what a gift it is they've been given?

The possibility of their own spark. The possibility to explore and actualize their humanity and their divinity. The opportunity to both struggle and strive and have a chance to figure it all out. And all those opportunities to learn about love, to learn how to be love, to learn how to love over the aches in this place. We have so little time here when it all comes down to it, something we often forget on a day to day basis so caught up in the circle that is life. But the truth is that everything alive will eventually die and that makes the span of our time finite and infinitely precious.

Many of us live life waiting for some kind of finale: a culmination of efforts that shows us it was all worth it. And hopefully the more we are in alignment with our truth of self, the more we do have immense moments of satisfaction that embody the art of living. But when it comes down to it, all we really have is right now. Today. We are not vowed or owed more.

I always believed I would have more time with Brent. More time to keep growing together, more time to make new memories, more time to build a greater foundation of connection and kindness in our later years. Now, there is a whole timeline that will never play out. We will not reminisce about our childhood as we grow older, or bury our parents together, or get to see who each other becomes 20 years from now; he will never grow past 39.

All we have is the time we had, and his loss has forced me to find the beauty and the gifts in what was. I don't get a do over.

As sad as this is, and admittedly it almost broke me down to the depths of my soul when my Dad brought out a small cake that said, *Happy 40ᵗʰ Birthday Brent*, there is good here too. The guts to live more authentically. The strength that comes as you realize you have faced your own grief and your parent's with an open heart and emotional integrity that left you smiling fondly at the last vestiges of the girl you once were, so you could fully step into the wise woman you have become.

Then find the courage to grab your life by the reigns and begin to change its course.

There is something that my brother said to me after he died that has kept the wind at my back, pushing me, ever since. He wasn't quite done when he first crossed over, so he drops by from time to time to share a few words. On one of these occasions, his voice rang so strongly, so out of nowhere in my mind, I knew what he had to say was of utmost import and that I needed to heed these words with every ounce of being.

If you knew my brother you would know he had a wicked sense of humor, could be perversely shocking, and he loved all the words. Especially the outrageous ones. And this was his essential, pressing advice about learning to cast off the doubts of what others might think and my own fears of failure, so I could find the courage to truly embrace and live my life:

Little Sister, you have to not give a fuck. Like a Mother Fucker. Goonies never say die kid. Chin up!

Happy Birthday Little Buddy. I'll see you in the stars.

64

REACH IN

for Mom

If you hold
your weeping mother
in your arms,
emptied by loss
of her son,
You will know the utter
humility of grief,
that sweeps away the ego
and levels the room with love,
And you will find the courage
to simply sit,
to hold a heart,
and reach in.
If you watch
your mourning father
choke—
on words unsaid,
You will know
the power of compassion
that trades grace
in place of judgment,
And you will find the courage
to let it be,
to hold space,
and reach in.
If you've ever found
yourself drowning,
in life's seas of loss,
gasping for all you're worth,
you will learn there
are three kinds of people
in this world:

Those who turn away
afraid to get their hands wet,
those who sit back and judge
how you drown,
and those who've already
learned life's golden mean
—that love will always
multiply in the places
where we see each other sink—
then take the time to extend
a helping hand
and reach in.
If you hold your
emptied mother
in your arms,
have her tell you
part of her heart left with him,
Then you know none
of it really matters,
except for the love
we have inside
and how we choose
to live it.
If you hold your
wanting heart
in your hands,
you will question less…
and ask more
of your sacred flame of life,
You will discover that you
ache from the same thing
that will become
your salvation:
that it is all love
and has always been love.
And you'll find the courage
to reach in.

65

FORGIVENESS

At some point, we are going to have to learn to forgive.

Some of us are walking around with losses and with timelines that were abruptly ripped from us and rife with jagged edges and unfinished business. We didn't get to say goodbye. We didn't get to say the things we wanted to say. We were in the middle of a book and the rest of the chapters got torn away, and we don't know how the story ends and refuse to find the ending life has given us a good enough "the end."

We may blame ourselves for the things we didn't do. We may blame them for the things they didn't do. We may blame the situation for being what it is. It is the truth that making peace with such abrupt unacceptability is like trying to make peace with the Ghost of Christmas Past where remembering becomes a haunted space and hindsight the greatest instigator of "I wish I would have."

It is also the truth that there will be things in this life that we find unacceptable. Things that seem senseless and horrible and without rhyme or reason. It is also the truth that if at some point, we don't become a relentless pursuant of our own right to have a peaceful heart, we will live forever at war with those ghosts.

Forgiveness goes a long way with all of this. With filing down the jagged edges by smoothing them away with self-compassion. With writing new endings to those books and turning them into stories on resilience and self-love. With releasing those who've gone before us to be free. *You have no more debt to me, I understand you did the best you could do*, we'll say. Or by releasing ourselves if we feel we're the ones in debt. *I lay down this burden, I did the best I could*, we'll say.

By realizing that every single one of us is only human, and as such is marked by the fallibility of mistakes, imperfections, and imperfect timing.

Forgive yourself for anytime you thought you didn't get it right and weren't enough. *My dear one, you have always been enough*; it's just that this world will make the best of us get it wrong, so we can learn to get it right. It is how we learn and grow and make our hearts bigger in this space.

Forgive them for anything they didn't get right, for they, like you, did not know how things would end and may have done it differently had they known. Instead, they did what they knew to do, and just like you, were learning, experiencing, and growing as they went.

Forgive the situation in its entirety. Take all of those bruises and callouses and ugly parts, and see they are just part of the palette of what makes us whole. Repurpose them as teachers and growing experiences, and do your best to cover them with love, for even that which is most ugly inside of any of us also deserves love.

Forgive this life for being what it is; there will be many mysteries that we do not understand. There is so much that is broken in this world, but there is joy too. For often it is we who are the wizards sitting behind the curtains spinning out the mad threads of these days, and we are also capable—oh so extraordinarily capable—of spinning out exquisite beauty.

Each of us learning about love as we go.

66

That's the thing about time.
It doesn't always heal things,
but it does change things.

Change things long enough, and you'll find yourself a million miles away
from where it all started.

Travel enough miles, and at some point,
when you didn't even notice its presence,
you just might find healing crept up, tapped you on the back,
and found you anyways.

In its own time.

67

GETTING RID OF RED

I have this thing for red colored clothing. Historically it is my favorite color, so I rarely get rid of anything that falls under the "shades of red" category, which in my generous classification ranges from anything light pink to deep rouge. I'll pull something from my closet to put in a donation bag and somehow find it mysteriously hanging back up the next day.

I can't possibly let go of this, I'll think. *It's my favorite color. I just can't.* Think a thought enough times, and it becomes a belief. Believe something long enough, and it becomes a value. Value something long enough, and it becomes a core value that goes unchallenged, so entwined it has become in our schema of who we think we are supposed to be.

Until Life makes you challenge it.

2016 has been a year of challenge. Like Life took everything that I believed, flipped it upside down, shook it up, and reshuffled all, sorting the wheat from the chaff. Loss will do that to a person; death reorders everything and purges the things in your life that really don't matter. The things that no longer suit. The stuff that keeps you small. The old fabrics of a younger self I was struggling to unweave.

Which is why yesterday I filled up two giant donation bags with almost all red clothing, carmine skirts, garnet tops and ruby shoes I've been hanging onto for years simply because of their color. It's part of my goal to slowly start donating, tossing and decluttering throughout the next year to help prepare us to move. We won't be taking much with us, best to start releasing now.

The thing about the sudden loss of someone you love is that you have the opportunity to learn about letting go from the ultimate teacher: death. Death can teach you radical lessons on detachment. Radical lessons on love. Radical lessons on learning to come to terms with an abrupt departure devoid of goodbyes. Radical lessons on acceptance, rebirth, and becoming.

We live life believing that certain things will be a constant in our lives until they no longer are, and my brother was one of those things. I never imagined that he wouldn't be here to see his 40th birthday, the possibility never entering my mind. Working on accepting his death has been a sorrowful, painful, and profound lesson that I can learn to let go of even the things I believed were tied to the core of who I am and how I see the world.

There are some things we will be asked to reconcile in this life that we deem irreconcilable. We learn to live with them anyways. Learn to make peace with the things that are crooked and misshapen and don't add up. Learn to make peace with the sudden, the inexplicable, the nonsensical.

Learn to make peace with those things, and you begin to learn the beautiful lessons of impermanence, transience, and the extreme importance of gratitude for the present moment; the finality of loss sharpening and heightening the gift of each breath. Learn to make peace with those things and you find the courage to step into a new version of self—letting go of obligations and image management and expectations of who you are supposed to be—so you can find the space and the courage to embody the person you believe you are becoming.

Learn to make peace with those things and you end up with a couple trash bags of crimson clothing that you're getting ready to chuck into the donation bin. Turns out I can get rid of red after all.

These days I often have an image that keeps reoccurring in my mind's eye. I see this wise woman dressed in colorful robes standing in the blue of sky. She is filled with openness and tenderness and a terrible compassion that simply loves over the imperfections of it all, and she is joyfully unraveling the threads of the tapestry before her. Unknotting, unwinding, untying; releasing them so they can find new places to weaves themselves into; knowing that every undoing is simply opportunity for new becoming.

She lets the red threads go, watching them fly merrily into the wind. Delighting at the absolute freeing of it all.

68

TANGLED

It can be a learning curve: self-compassion. It goes against the way society has shaped our grain and the voice of the inner critic who rings with authority and shame inside, yet we have to try our best to learn not to judge our own process of life and loss. We are our own worst enemies, placing expectations upon our shoulders of where we think we should be in the process, how we should feel, and what it should look like.

*H*owever, you are going to find as you travel further and further along that things are going to look very differently than you expected. This is not because you are somehow doing it wrong, this is because Life is not a linear process and neither are we. You are not going to travel on an upward trajectory where you just get "better and better" as you move away from the point of grief. Instead, you are going to find that the grief process is a tangled mass of yarn that you slowly try and untangle, integrating complex feelings, new experiences, and what it means to lose.

This is why there are so many ups and down, so many good days and bad days, so many times where you go down the rabbit hole of loss. And you will find as this string begins to untangle that there are more days that start to feel smoother and even, but the knots will still be there, and when you encounter them they will require your attention.

That's why it all looks so tangled—because there are many knots along the way you didn't anticipate, didn't see coming, didn't expect. Years can pass, and you will still find there are some knots you encounter and are still working out how to untangle. It doesn't have to look a certain way. It doesn't have to all be unraveled. There was a start point when the loss happened, but there is no time limit for a finish. Maybe it takes the rest of your life to keep untangling those knots. You do a little bit of work, lay it down for awhile, pick it back up when life brings it to your attention again.

Some processes operate on a timeline of their own accord and will keep on going until the going is done. *Oh well.* As long as you are listening to your heart, giving yourself permission to feel what you feel and doing your best to keep moving through it, you're doing all right. And if you're not doing those things? *Oh well!* You're still doing all right, for being human can be terribly difficult and lonely, and we are all navigating things as best we know to do without an instruction manual.

And the greatest gift you can give yourself in this process is to trade self-judgment for kindness and be merciful to yourself wherever you are at. Judgment is only going to make it worse and make those knots feel even tighter and more resolute, but kindness with its forgiving touch and gentle ways, has a way of loosening everything and helping it relax and just be where it's at.

Even the most tangled of things.

69

*I have learned that when you finally get to
the end of the line of judgment–*

*When you can take it no further,
have exhausted your supply of opinions
and objections and should have beens–*

*Have thrown your hands up in the air,
realizing Life can be a real mess,
and there but the grace of Love go any of us–*

You will find compassion waiting there.

70

HELLO, GOODBYE

There is this race through the city of Anchorage that has me running towards the solstice sun rising over the mountains at 7:30 this morning. It is an under the radar kind of race, today isn't about accomplishment, it is about trilogy. I've run it the past two summers and with this being my last summer here, it somehow seemed fitting to give it a go one last time, a goodbye of sorts.

*R*ight now, everything feels like a goodbye of sorts. Or at least the beginning of goodbye. I have the sense that there are new hellos on the other side of this chute of transition, it's just that they are very faint. I'm not quite close enough yet to hear them.

Things are changing. I feel it in my cells, this sense that everything is unlacing and loosening as if Life is unspooling itself around me. A product of our upcoming move next year, the loss of my brother, my fears over my mother's health; how much longer do we have?

Most days I feel like I'm holding space, keeping time, doing things to keep life spinning as I wait for the clock to wind down before we leave, wait for the resolution or conclusion to something I can't quite put to words. It's a feeling inside, anticipation of the cusp of change. I'm not quite ready to jump but no longer have the option to go back, so I hang there suspended, waiting for the last of the threads holding me to unwind.

I keep time as I run. Past emerald trees, over long streams, up dusty roads, and down earthen trails. I have hours to keep time with my steps, right foot, left foot, over and over again, each step taking me farther away from where I just was, each step taking me closer towards: one two, one two, hello, goodbye.

There is a Buddhist word for being in a place of transition, an intermediate state, *Bardo*. Literally, it references the belief that a liminal state can occur when a soul has left this life and not yet reincarnated into the next so their spirit waits in transition between two lives on earth, the last one and the next. Metaphorically it is used to signify a transitory state where life is suspended for awhile, and opportunities for spiritual growth arise as external constraints diminish.

I am in *Bardo* as I wait on my cusp of change. Something about the loss of my brother, my concern for my mother, the expectancy of the move to Kauai has given me permission to step away from external constraints and get down to the heart of what really matters.

I decide to run for love today. I run for my brother, I run for my family, I run for all the grief and resilience we've found. I run for grace, I run for peace, I run for all the untold stories of hurt people carry inside. I run and think of my best friend—my husband—already way ahead of me on the course, and I reflect on how a silly picture he posted of myself on a bike garnered almost 100 social media likes, while the picture of his father's grave received so little attention.

I run and wonder why it is so hard for us to start seeing what's real? When we started valuing shiny over soul? When we lost the ability to reach out and offer kindness and support on the things that matter most? How we lost the language of love and compassion that extends care in the places people hurt?

After awhile, I'm the one who hurts. Something pulling in my hip, something wrong with my toe. I find it harder to keep my pace and start running to support people. I stop and chat to those who are walking, learn that it is Olivia's first marathon and the guy from Louisiana will complete his "50 marathons in 50 states" goal here, today. I offer "good jobs!" and smiles when I can. I hurt, but I'm happy to be out here with so many stories, so many people. Sometimes I fall behind, sometimes I'm the one passing: one two, one two, hello, goodbye.

I wistfully think of my house as I run past the part of the trail that shoots off to it. I think about moving in a year, finally the perfect cottage home for our family filled with visions of rainbows and gardens and whimsy; I'm so attached, and we'll be leaving it behind.

I think about the courage it takes to jump and release so many structures: the job, the income, the home, the social groups, the familiarity, the comfort zone. I think of my mom and wonder what will be. Think of how much this past year has changed me. Think of how my heart now feels so tired, so huge, so old, so newly born. All at the same time.

The last mile gets closer, and I'm grateful to be close, ready to be done. I keep time for the home stretch, knowing that sometimes all we can do is keep time in our lives as we leave what has passed behind in order to move in the direction of towards. I see the finish chute, remember it's the last time my feet will pass this way, that these steps have been another passage on the journey.

Make my feet carry me one last stretch: one two, one two, hello, goodbye.

71

WILDFLOWERS

There will always be a hole the shape of the loss inside your heart that cannot be filled by anyone or anything.

*E*ach life is a unique imprint upon this planet, of course we cannot fill or replace or just get over one another when someone has exited our lives, nor should we heap expectation upon ourselves to try. People who do not understand the nature of loss may not understand how it can hurt so much after all this time, but I say a hole in the heart will always hurt and to treat our losses with casual expendability—to deny their ever changing impact—is to deny what it means to be most human.

It will always feel like a nuclear bomb went off somewhere inside of me the day my brother died. And it's not that the fact of that bomb has become less potent, but more that as time spins on, I have begun to see new life finding the courage to grow around the site of the blast.

Wildflowers begin to pop their heads up with stubborn hope. A few birds fly by reminding me the world is bigger than just this space, and life will always carry on. I see the resilience in the soil that is finding a way to keep living despite the waste done here. A tree begins to grow again; she's got unshakable roots, for she's withstood some of the worst life has to offer and still found a way to believe in the sky and rise towards the strength of the sun.

No. It is not that any of us will ever, ever forget whosoever touched our lives and left them too soon. It is more that time offers the necessary seeds of nourishment for us to remember our roots. Slowly grow our way out of the desperate dark of devastation and find the heart-growing grit to look up and receive the sunlight.

72

THE COLLECTORS

They are drops in a salmon sea,
this collection of moments
that compose
our days—
Each of us collecting the love
we have come here to learn.
I watch life rise:
an opening of heart and joy
and strings of feral roses...
only to watch it fade to tangerine twilight,
so it can set, then learn
to open when time
once more.
Everything a season, each open a closing,
each end a beginning,
each love that passes through our lives
a gateway for growth.
And do you see that it is
all a miracle, all a privilege
to be a collector of this
time and space?
A gatherer of each coral bloom
and peach swept set;
a taker of this Grace called Life;
a giver of all we collect.
Because we are just passing through,
standing on the stars,
scooping the moments into us,
watching the Love
go by.

73

SPHERE

If you sit with the not fair long enough you will discover there are two choices in life. Bitterness and Disillusion or Compassion and Love.

*A*nd while having moments of the former is inevitable, the later is what I keep striving for. Striving for finding this sort of radical, fierce compassion for the whole.

Striving to use my heart and not my ego. To step beyond the not fair of Brent's death. To step outside of the situation, see the brokenness and the resilience in my grieving parents, see those things in myself. To see the situation as a giant sphere filled with awful and beauty and grief and healing and unfair and hope and hate and love. To see how opposing truths can occupy the same space and make peace among themselves.

To walk around that sphere looking at the different viewpoints without judgment, without the need to fix, see how they are all connected, how they work together. To see how love binds the whole thing together, even when it doesn't feel like it.

If I take a step even further away, the sphere gets bigger. Filled with the people I know, the people I don't know, the people who inhabit this space together. Who are all working out their own sense of brokenness and resilience, as they try and find the love that binds it together. Each in their own way. There is exquisite wonder in that sphere if you learn to see it. Even with all the cracks and pain, it offers the potential to step back, look at the whole of who we are, and find the beauty in the full sphere of being human.

And if you learn to stare at that sphere long enough, you begin to focus less on how unfair things are and begin to focus more on finding the Same Love that holds us all together, in spite of and because of, ourselves. Because that's the crux of the Energy of Love: we don't have to do anything to merit it. It is already Is. Equally available to everything and all.

We just have to learn to sit in its circle and receive.

74

FOREVER

There were times where part of me felt like all I wanted to do was stay in a state of depression and grief. But all along, the wiser part of me knew there was a lesson in Love to be learned from all of it, and my job was to decide whether or not I wished to receive it. Whether or not I was going to choose to let the sunlight do its work and warm the dark places inside of me.

*W*hether or not I was going to close myself off to the hurt of this world or find the absolute courage to open my heart just a little bit farther and receive. Receiving meant turning my attention from what I had lost to become cognizant of what I had gained. Receiving meant letting go of *what was* to accept something greater in *what is*.

What is turns out to be a massive recognition that you can remove the material and earthly realm of a relationship, but you cannot touch that which we hold in our heart. I believe this to be Love in its purest, most divine form. Just because you can no longer see its physical manifestation when something has passed, doesn't mean it's not there, and as long as you hold love in your heart, those who've passed are only a heartbeat away.

And if you can grasp that concept, truly grab onto it letting it envelop you with an unalloyed truth that burns through all but that which is most genuine and true, then you realize even though everything has changed, absolutely nothing has changed. They will always be with us: forever. The energy of love cannot be reduced, it only continues to multiply every time we realize and express it.

I cloak myself in this knowledge: you can lose a life, but you can't lose love. Let it make me stand strong and straight and realize: I am not a broken being after all. I am a walking container of all the love I've collected. Big and strong and full of life.

The love that ripped me apart, is the same love reknitting my seams. Love has become my revolution and my absolution.

75

PEACEMAKER

You have to
learn to make peace
with it, all of it—

Even the things
that don't
feel peaceful,
even the
unanswered questions,
even the
unanswered life
that you are busy
trying to live.

It doesn't all
have to equate
or fit together
or logically
add up.

It just has to
be whatever
you've got
to give in any
given moment,
and whenever
you offer that—

Make peace that
it's enough.

76

BETTER DAYS

I spent part of my morning looking through a photo album from about 6 summers ago. Life was in an entirely different place then, on the cusp of extreme change, though I hadn't yet realized it.

*M*ost of the pictures are myself in motion. Climbing something. Biking somewhere. Racing this and running that. Tapping into previously unexpressed energy inside that taught me how strong, clever and brave I could be—I don't think you can run up and down a mountain for speed and time and not tap into those attributes within yourself.

I didn't know at the time those were the same attributes I would need 6 months later when I found the courage to speak the words that would leave me starting over on my own, even though I didn't know how to be alone, how to support myself, how to do life solo.

But I was strong and brave and clever.

The girl who climbed more mountains than I could count multiple times a week. The girl who cruised up and down monstrous hills on her road bike. The girl who had never done a triathlon in her life, then found herself with an Ironman medal around her neck precisely one year after starting training.

The girl who was strong and brave and clever.

The girl who trained for an ultra in the heart of an Alaskan winter by doing solo runs at sub-zero temperatures for several hours on end; water bottle freezing up, eyelashes icing with frost, running through chilly winds and chunks of ice and trails that crunched with arctic cold. By the time race day wound around, I found out that 40 miles on April, Oregonian, deep forest trails were a snap compared to the conditions I had trained.

Strong and brave and clever, the girl.

The girl who grabbed my life by the reigns and had an unshakeable faith in my ability to be my own change, even when my own faith in self faltered. SHE believed in me so profoundly, how could I possibly let that part of myself down? So I made the changes she insisted upon. I started over.

My brother is alive in those days. He's scattered throughout the photo album; it's bittersweet. I'm reminded as I look through the pages that during that time period he had severe blood clotting and ended up in the ICU over Christmas. The doctors told him it was a miracle he was alive. After that, he took medication daily. Monitored his blood levels. Tried to live better. At least for awhile. As time went on everything seemed under control with the clots. Fine tuned and managed, he didn't think much more of it. I guess last January proved that wrong.

I have wondered what he would have changed over the last 6 years if he knew they would be the last 6 of his life. How he might change his story if he knew there wasn't going to be many opportunities for better days ahead, that the days he was living each day were the better days.

That each of us is spinning out our stories each and every day and that these days, *these days right now*, are the days we have to look to for better. Have to find the beauty in. Have to see the light of soul's becoming, even in the face of dark. That each day that offers breath is one more day of better. We just don't always have the eyes to see, which has a lot less to do with looking with the mind and more to do with listening with the heart.

I see the beauty in the pictures as I look back. Time, wisdom, and perspective all help me see the better of those days where smiling eyes and frantic fun often hid the breaking heart and growing spirit emerging within. I see the girl who is about to dive into the deep end and find out what it truly means to live an authentic life where her life will align with her inner truth.

I spent yesterday in the mountains. Mt. Marathon; one of the ones I used to race up and down for speed back in those days where I was the girl. Yesterday was just for fun though as I've found the longer I've embodied being strong, brave, and clever by living an authentic life, the less I've needed my old platforms of courage. I've learned to see living life as my truest self, by fearlessly plunging into my soul, as the greatest act of courage I can offer in this world. My platform has become my heart. There is much space to run free.

I climb with an old friend; cool air, shifting fog, occasional glimpses of sun. The trails are familiar, the conversation laced with laughter, the sky performing a filmy dance of clouds that keeps the views of the peaks across the bay ever changing.

I feel the old days course through me as I run down; shale flying, dust in my face, legs pounding. I feel the spirit of my brother; I don't feel him as often these days, but he is here this day running down, remembering, feeling the presence of the day—the better—with me. There's no audience, no clock, no timer. Nothing but open skies, an almost empty mountain, true friendship and my becoming.

It is the best run on the mountain I've ever had.

77

FIREWEED BREEZE

There is something good running
through the veins of these days.
The peonies riot over cool glasses of lemonade,
while the ghosts that we knew drift... on past.
Pausing to say *Hello* through the breeze,
on violet stretch of fireweed.

I keep searching for you across
orange clouds, looking for bright popsicle
dreams on the horizon that tell me,
You are There,
and I am Here.
Finding the good in the sounds
of the lavender trees, holding back
the dissolution of night with the bright
of a mid summer's day.

There is something good running
through the veins of these days.
The bumblebees buzz
—*buzz, buzz, buzz*—
and I roll myself into the arctic roses
declaring a war of color after a season
slashed with gray. I wish to wash myself
in their scene and scent,
dare this world
to show me ugly in the face of my bold bloom.
No dark can touch my soft of beauty,
see how I blossom
in the face of despair?
You were all I always knew,

we were young and so much free.
Star Wars and Make Believe
and Hide & Seek and
Mario and Summer Time and School Days
and Chocolate Cake and Growing Up and Growing Big
and In Between—
always, You and Me.

There is something good running
through the veins of these days.
Life and Love and Time and Death,
and it's all so finite I want to
pull it into me
and weave myself into the change,
shouting with the birds on the high pink trees
—*peace, peace, peace—*
carrying their notes of joy
into the streams of hope
that float above, telling us to *look up!*
—and remember just how much grace
is running through the heartbeat
of this place.

I know you believed I left:
I never did.
We got older and
I needed to fly like those birds on the streams
and I know I changed it up on us
and Things were different and
once We were young and
then We weren't and…

Adulthood can seem a terrible truth to be.

But the Truth is,
I was always there and
You were always in my heart and

the Love never changed and
I wish you would have let me in and
You finally got it right towards the end
and then You left and…
Now I am forced to live my truth in reverse,
find you in the blush on the trees.

There is something good running
through the veins of these days.
It's all changing on me
like the thrum of a June beat,
that beats— — —
like the bloom of that lavender tree.
Soft purple parcel and fragrant face,
fleeting and fleeing;

July into August to Fall
and then Again;
I'm still and spent, outside and in,
all in one moment, watching myself spin
in those solstice weaves…
as the ghosts that I knew drift on past.

And I want to hug you into me,
bury you in the only place
I know you'll be safe,
so I can birth you out in every word
and breath and love and beat,
as long as
you're *There*
and I'm *Here.*

Keep you alive on my fireweed breeze.

78

BRAMBLES AND ROSES

There is always joy among the sorrow and roses among the brambles.

*O*ur emotional experience isn't relegated to just one thing when it comes to loss. It is relegated to all emotions joined together by the word "and," helping us hold both love and grief side by side in our hearts.

Part of grieving is the work of clearing the brambles, pulling them out in thorny lots and dealing with the pricks and wounds where they've made us bleed as we allow ourselves the time and space to mend and heal. Our roses are never any lesser for the brambles, but we will find that when we clear them out, the roses become even more pristine, pure, distilled. Our enjoyment of the rose that much more intense, because we know the stinging rub of the brambles.

And when you know the sting of the thorn, you learn to value those roses with a ferocity of gratitude that can only come from learning about pain from the inside out. Life's gifts become a testament to grace when we have experienced the knowledge of the wound. Grief then becomes the catalyst for distilled joy. Sorrow a doorway for goodness. The work of the heart—in this space of loss—to acknowledge all the beauty and all the ugliness in this world.

Then join them together by the AND.

79

MEANT

Despite my protestations,
he told me it was always supposed
to look this way.
Like the quiet that comes after
the rain fall,
the inevitable light that chases
the break of night,
the melt of a grilled cheese on
the stick of a hot summer's day.
Some things are just meant.
Nobody ever promised
life would be a certain something
or guaranteed our breaths
beyond today—
we were just told to learn
about love.
To lose ourselves in the
sapphire seam where sea become sky;
forget the illusion of isolation;
shed bittersweet tears over how
achingly connected
it all is.
To realize our humanity
in the same breath that avers
our divine.
To learn to trust the process,
even when it doesn't go a thing
like we expect.

Like the palmy breeze offering
a respite of hope when all else

goes still,
the punch of bright stars that knock out
the black of winter's sky,
the incandescent way you will
forever be a part of me:
Some things are just meant.

80

BLOOM

There are times in this world that all we can see is the gray and the storm and the clouds. We lose our sense of warmth and almost forget that the sunshine still exists. It is during these times that it is hardest to trust, to remember Life is still on our side and that we are not alone in this.

*W*hen I look back on some of the toughest chapters of my life, I now know that, even if I didn't see it at the time, Life always found a way to see me through. Even on the hardest days when the sky did fall and I was surrounded by broken pieces and "where do I go from here's," I still came out the other side.

When we can't see the sun through the clouds, it is easy to forget that Life will not abandon us if we stay the course. Life will not forsake us if we move through it with sincere intent. Life will support us in becoming our authentic selves. Sometimes this means we just keep moving forward, every day a step in a new direction that will eventually reveal a beautiful destination.

Sometimes this means we take deep breaths and keep trying to bring ourselves back to a space of love every time we feel lost. And sometimes this means we will be asked to step blindly into an unknown we do not understand, nor can see our way through, and the best we can do is keep trying to trust that new life will be waiting on the other side.

Life doesn't bring us to the edge in order to abandon us to the darkness, Life brings us here so we can learn to make a way for more light. For without the light, we will never find what we need to bloom.

81

THE GOLDEN PARACHUTE

Since this is my last summer in Alaska, I have found myself wanting to experience as much of the state as I can before the opportunity is gone, which is how I found myself up in Tok this weekend sitting at a restaurant called Fast Eddy's, surrounded by an odd crew of ragged travelers.

*T*he parking lot is full of giant RV's, dusty cars packed to the brim with camping and fishing gear, and plenty of Canadian plates since we are less than 100 miles from the border of Yukon Territory. Over dinner I enjoy a salmon burger and curly fries along with the eclectic mix of people as I wonder what their stories might be. As I sit there it occurs to me that with a move planned, our time in Alaska is limited, and I may never be back by way of Tok again.

Remember this moment, remember this realized possibility, I keep saying to myself. *Cherish it, for time is finite, and this may be the only time you ever pass through this place.*

It is a strange and curious thing to realize the limitations of time. When we are younger it all seems endless, spanning on towards forever. But as we get older we begin to realize there are some things we will never do again, some places we will not return to, some passages we will not retake.

I turn 39 this week and in living *Life After Brent* this past year, life has taken on a precious quality. I try and take little for granted. He never made it past 39 and, Life willing, I will. That means every step forward becomes a golden parachute, an unexpected opportunity that some people don't have. Now I age for both him and for me, remembering that there are no guarantees when it comes to tomorrow, just the guarantee of this moment, today.

These days it is all a gift. All of it sacred. All of it a privilege to breathe and learn and grow and love and hurt and fail and find the joy. Of course, there are the mundane moments: the moments of struggle and being human and having down days. But I am finding that even in these there is still something sacred to be found. That as long as we are *here*, there are always opportunities for the up days, always opportunities to grow from our experiences.

Losing my brother has taken away the assumptions about how life should look. I make plans as best I can, even as I accept that Life sometimes has its own plans that take us in another direction entirely. Trying to pretend we somehow have control is the equivalent of saying we can hold the ocean in our grasp: it is but an illusion.

These days I continue to focus on the only thing I do have control over. Myself. My heart. My thoughts. The state of my own internal affairs. I can't change what has happened, but I can learn to make peace with what has come to pass.

Make peace with the part of myself who has this terrible wisdom that we were never really in charge to begin with. Make peace with the part of myself who has come to learn that death is just another door. Make peace with the part of myself that still rages and screams and howls at the moon over the unfairness of it all. Make peace with all the imperfect parts. Make peace with the part who just wants to find the love that knits it all together.

Make peace with the fact that balance is unobtainable, that the best I can do is learn to sink into and embrace wherever I should find myself on any given day. Make peace with the fact that I was never promised life would look a certain way; I was only promised this chance to pass through this world at this particular point in time.

These days I shake my head at all the sadness this world has to offer, open my heart to all the beauty there is to find. Remember we were never really in control to begin. Learn to accept its imperfections. Howl when it's unfair, smile when it's golden. Find the love that smooths our ragged edges. Learn to sink into and embrace whatever I find on any given day.

And on this day, I happen to find myself surrounded by acres of pines and rolling ridges and a silty river snaking its way through the cool of up north. Rain patters on our little orange tent as the dogs curl between our sleeping bags, and I fall asleep listening to the music of the water. For one night it is golden, and I find myself terribly limited, unable to hold onto all the beauty and love.

So I let it wash through me instead, snake its way through my heart like the cool river streaming nearby; polishing, eroding, and changing my shape as water is given to do. *Remember this moment, remember this realized possibility. Cherish it, for time is finite, and this may be the only time you ever pass through this place.*

I want to hang onto the moment, keep it with me for as long as I can, but when the time comes to say goodbye I let it go instead. Say goodbye to the space of today, so I can move on to tomorrow. And in the end, it doesn't matter if I return this way or not—I'm staring 39 squarely in the eye and, Life willing, I have the golden parachute of moving forward.

It is more than my brother had so I carry him with me as I go, figuring as long as I'm moving forward I really have all I need. We were never promised life would look a certain way, we were only promised a chance for now.

We are just passing through the walls of this place. Freeing each other as we go.

82

THE LAVENDER TREE

They said it was the day
all energies shift—
Where dark becomes light,
where fear becomes hope,
and all that we carry in the grave of our hearts
continues to be laid to rest
among the feet
of new bloom.
You can't erase the fall
of the lavender tree—
they cut off her limbs, unthinking,
not knowing they had been my friends;
my wishes for better days twined
to each branch with soft pleas,
earnest thoughts,
and kind prayers.
Nor can you make the peonies
stand tall once more:
last moon a crush of color
these days a collapse of fade.
But the fuchsias are afire draping purple
and carmine all over the earth
reminding me
not all the wild things are gone,
they still hide in unlooked nooks,
awaiting discovery.
And the sun is still pushing high,
singing a song of triumph over the dark,
daring me to skirt his brazen gaze,
forcing me to look up
and bask...

in the certainty that all things
have a time, each moment a place,
and us a place among it
All.
I can't erase the fall of the lavender tree—
I still speak to her as if she were there,
tell her I'll see her again,
in time.
But I can let those gripping graves
rest… and fall into the balm of season.
And when it is time for dark to be light,
for fear to be hope, for life to go on,
I can let if all shift—
Towards love.

83

SACRED

I had this realization this week that life, in all its shapes and forms and moods, is all spiritual.

We have this tendency when we are being our better selves— our loving, kinder, gentler, more patient selves—to feel like we are being good. The best version of self. More presentable and acceptable. More spiritual in a sense.

While I am all for continuing to learn how to access our better selves and reach towards our own sense of light, I am coming to realize that we lose so much that is authentic, real, and raw; we lose so many opportunities to practice self-love, and in return to learn to better love others, when we invalidate the experiences of self that feel ugly, dark, and less.

Self-love is the fundamental footstep to the sacred path. It is a path that we are all on, whether or not we are aware of it—all of us trying to return to a space of love, all of us seeking love to help heal the wounds in our lives. And the only way we can learn to find self-love is to embrace all our moments. The beautiful ones. The ambivalent ones. The ones where we are sitting at the back of Life's Class angry, and churlish, and scowling.

This past year has taught me what cessation truly means. After he was gone, I vividly remember realizing that my brother no longer had the chance to be anything more than what he'd been. He no longer had the chance for great. He no longer had the chance to blow it. He no longer had the chance to choose good or choose bad or create his own labels as to what those things mean.

He didn't have the chance to move to Hawaii, or to look for a new job, or to play video games with his friends, or to sleep in too long, or to cheer for his cherished Patriots, or to eat prime rib, or to have an extra bowl of rocky road, or to yell at me, or to love me, or to open presents on Christmas, or to watch Lord of the Rings together, or to see the next Star Wars, or to know what his future would hold.

To have good days and bad days, sorrow and joy. He didn't have the chance to strive for new possibilities. He didn't have the chance to roll in the mud and be stuck and wait for things to turn a corner. He didn't have the chance to choose to live in shadow until he found his way out. He didn't have the chance to choose to revel in and embrace the grace of light. We no longer had the chance to be better or worse than what we were.

That is the meaning of cessation to me: the realization of how absolutely finite it all is.

And in that sense of finite, I have begun to see how sacred is the whole journey, because if we are HERE—here in the beautiful, difficult, finite, possible space of this place—it means we have chances. Choices. Possibilities. Regardless of what we choose to do with them.

And chances, choices, and possibilities are an inherent gift. Inherently holy, and hallowed, and precious, and cherished, and prayerful, and revered, and sublime, and divine, and all the words that usually get relegated to religion, but really shouldn't, because they are simply adjectives that describe the gift of being HERE and the Opportunities that are our lives.

That is what I mean when I say it is all spiritual, all sacred, and though I definitely prefer some moments to others, I can no longer separate one moment from the other and judge it as better or worse, more valid or less valid, more spiritual or dark when I have begun to see the gift itself *is the whole*.

Even in my murky waters of self, I am learning to embrace what I am feeling and see it for the gift it is: to be so utterly human—to be in the space of HERE—that I can revel in those murky waters and have the experience of feeling them. Of choosing where to go from there.

We were never wrong. We were never bad. And even in our darkest of places, there is always something divine to be found.

It is all spiritual. All sacred. All a chance to Love.

84

BIG

I don't want to do this anymore.

How many of us have uttered these words during a time of heartache, where our instinct is to emotionally go curl up in a fox hole, lick our wounds, and wall ourselves off from the constant stream of pain? But the thing is, we didn't come here to build up walls, we came here to tear them down.

People can try and save themselves from potential depth of feeling, of loving, of losing. We can try and eschew attachment, "I will never let myself care so much about anyone again, this hurts too much," and keep love at a distance. We can try and hold ourselves back and trade barricaded interactions for heartfelt connection, but I suspect that at the end of the day even the best attempts at defending the human heart will backfire, leaving those who avoid meaningful connection feeling more and more like an empty shell of self.

And in the end, despite our paltry efforts, most likely our hearts are going to try to do what they came here to do anyways: Love. They have a language all their own you see, and they can't help but seek ways to speak it.

So if you have loved and life has handed you buckets of heartbreak—find that fox hole for awhile if need be. Stop and get off the merry-go-round for a bit if it helps. Cocoon yourself in a blanket fort. Curl up into the cradle of life. Let yourself be scooped by something bigger than just yourself. Take all the time you need with this. Quit as often as you like in this process. Honor what you are feeling until it's worked its way through your system; I can't tell you how many times I told Life "I quit" throughout the years, sometimes we need to contract for awhile before we are ready to expand.

However, in all my quittings, I have learned that Life is big enough for my quit. Big enough for my hate. Big enough for my rage. Big enough for my despair and exhaustion and bewilderment over how hard it can be to be human. And I have begun to realize that no matter how many times we quit life, Life will never quit on us. Life will always respect our need for contraction and support us in unseen ways as we rest, all while waiting at the ready, with arms wide open, for the time we choose to expand once more.

If we came here to be BIG, to shine bright, to reach our full potential, then we must know that it takes more courage to open our hearts back up after hurt than it does to put up walls, and Life always responds to our courage. Our world will only be as big and beautiful as we allow it to be.

Opening and closing in proportion to the worlds we create in our hearts.

85

I'm Just Not Myself

We are not meant to stay the same person for the entirety of our lives. In fact, hard as they may seem, emotional growth and spiritual change are exactly what we came here for.

I left 38 a different person than I started it, and now I find myself in an invisible space of transition at the beginning of 39. A blackout of sorts, where I can't quite see the bigger picture to even begin to describe my scene. Mostly I just feel the shifts, living life in an undefinable space—not quite where I want to go, far from where I used to be—seeing where life chooses to grow like the great, green trees I see outside.

When I was younger, I was scared of these shifts, living under the pretense that I was always supposed to have a sense of status quo of self; supposed to return to a core set point every time I was knocked out of equilibrium. *I'm sorry, I'm just not myself,* I'd say, as if this was some terrible thing that needed to be remedied immediately. And now I know that those words—*I'm just not myself*—are always an invitation from life to grow into a new set point of self and leave the old status quo behind.

I can't say I always love it, being in that invisible space of transition, but I can say I've learned to recognize and embrace the space of not knowing when it comes to the possibility of tomorrow. I do know where I'll be tomorrow, but I don't know quite who I'll be. And there is great relief and release in accepting the undefinable process over the certainty of knowing.

There are times we have to breathe the change. To find our answers among the living of the questions, let ourselves be out of sorts for a bit, learn to turn each time the winds come, sift through the pieces that no longer belong and find a new set point along the way. Times where the most fitting, beautiful, honest, embracing words we can utter as we work through our own evolution of self, not quite the person we once were, not quite the person we're yet to be—

I'm just not myself.

86

INDOMITABLE

My dear girl,
there were a million times
you could have given up
this past year.

You thought it would look
a certain way,
then it didn't.

But I will tell you a secret
—*you were never alone*—
and no matter how far
down you felt in that water...
there was always solid ground
inside of you.

Don't you see?

You have tied your
indomitable heart to the binds
of Love
and will always find
your way back home.

For whatsoever has been
touched by Love,
nothing will ever tear
asunder.

GRIEF'S RELEASE

We will spend the rest of our lives letting go of those we've grieved, in a constant dance of releasing and receiving that teaches us—where the old has passed away, Life will always bring the grace of new.

87

The next four pieces were written during Fall 2013 and Fall 2014. They are dedicated to anyone who has ever lost a beloved pet.

I. FOR THE LOVE OF AN OLD DOG

Dog is getting old. I see it in the way he moves, I can feel it when he breathes, I sense it in his soulful eyes that gently say, though he still has time left, his time is indeed coming.

*E*very morning that he wakes up with his old man cough, little tail wagging, snuffling and shuffling on the bed to tell me it's time to go out—because when you are old, the need to go suddenly becomes more urgent—I am grateful for another day with my best friend. He knows everything about me, loves me anyway, and though he can't speak back, Dog has other ways of communicating through his licks and cuddles that let me know how loved I am.

The feeling is mutual. He is seldom left behind on my adventures and doesn't seem to understand that while I take him to as many places as I can, there are some places he is not allowed to go. He has a hard time comprehending this, his liquid gaze reminding me that I am his pack and where I go, he thinks he should too.

At work he is my co-therapist, making people smile with his gremlin like appearance, curling up by clients as they share the deepest matters of their hearts. He contributes his own wise energy to the office; his old age reminding people to slow down, rest, and consider that despite the concerns of the moment, ultimately we are all participants in the cycles and seasons of life and our lives are short and precious. For someday, we too shall be old, like Dog.

I met Dog back in 2003 when I was living in Flagstaff, Arizona and he was living in Austin, Texas. I found him on a rescue site—took one look at his Yoda-Gizmo hybrid of a face—and said, "That's my Dog." It didn't matter that he was in another state; one adoption application and a plane flight later, he was mine.

We bonded quickly, but Dog came with his own dog sized set of baggage. Scared of people; often lashing out with aggressive growls and occasional bites; fearfully dodging limbs and feet; and scarfing down food as if he never had enough, I wondered what stories of woe he may carry from his first four years of life.

He made the move from Arizona to Alaska and resided with me in a time and place that feels long ago and far away as I write these words. At the time, he had a family of two to protect, a house to guard, and despite all his flaws, he was a very, very good Dog. I thought my love for him couldn't possibly grow any more, and I used to cry at the thought of losing him someday, telling myself, "He is only 6, only 7, only 8. He has lots of life left. Don't think about such things."

But things really changed for Dog and I when he saw me through a divorce and moved with me into a new home with a new roommate and new animals. Though they stayed upstairs and we stayed downstairs, he would lie in bed staring suspiciously at the ceiling as he heard the patter of other furry feet, looking at me in question, asking me why he had gone from being the only Dog of a secure home to living in this new place with strange sounds, smells, and creatures.

Our space was tiny; he no longer had a big house to roam. He laid close to me every night listening to the sounds of my tears, absorbing my every mood—the fears, the griefs, the anxious excitement about the brave new world, the vast ache in my heart and blank emptiness that spanned my insides as I wondered if time really would heal all wounds. He was a solid ball of reassurance as I learned what it was like to sleep alone.

At some point, the boundaries Dog and I had in the previous chapter of life began to blur. Instead of staying home during the daytime, he started not only coming to work but almost everywhere I went. Dog's life had been interrupted—he didn't want to stay in a home that wasn't his. I had become his home, and truth be told, I needed Dog as much as he needed me.

My old Dog began to learn new tricks in our new life. He had once shown aggression to other animals but slowly mellowed and learned to coexist with two cats and another dog in our rental space. He once hated to be touched by strangers but now sought pats from people. He met new people, and went to new places, and saw that the world was much bigger than the former house he occupied.

Dog changed and grew in our uncharted new world. So did I.

He is sleeping much longer and heavier as of late. He is walking slower, taking longer to make it up and down the stairs, often relying on me lifting him. Our walks have become short meanders; making it all the way around the duck pond without being carried is reason to celebrate. Cataracts makes it harder to see. Sometimes I call him and he just stands there looking addled, as if he's forgotten who and what he is about. He is coughing more. The vet didn't find anything wrong, it appears that Dog is just old.

And that's the rub of it: Dog is old. We had a discussion on his 14th birthday that this year was going to be a great year of life. I lovingly held him and told him that I am planning on lots of life left for him, but if he realizes his time is coming then he needs to let me know, so I can prepare both myself and him for when it is time to let go.

I am hoping he is one of those scrappy dogs who defies statistics and makes it to 18 or 19 years, for though he is showing signs of age, he is a healthy Dog. Yet despite my wistful hopes, I am faced with the reality my best friend may not be with me much longer. And I am prepared to make that transition when the time comes.

No longer the young twenty something girl who once cried at the unbearable thought of losing Dog, I am now the woman who lives the reality that his time is coming, and I will have great grief, for I have loved him as dearly as I have loved a person. To me, this is friendship and unconditional love. Just because it comes in furry form doesn't make it less real.

It will be a tremendous loss, but I have seen loss. And I have made it through. I now know exactly what I am made of, and I have gained some measure of wisdom that makes me realize there are cycles to life, natural ebbs and flows, that must happen. We do not know joy if we do not know sorrow. We do not know what wholeness feels like if we have not known brokenness. We do not know true, quenching love if we have not had pale imitations that leave us thirsting for more.

And we do not know life if we do not know death.

And when you've seen the death of something or someone? Then you learn that after death there is rebirth. You learn that the deepest wounds you never thought would heal do indeed heal, if you find the courage to face them. You learn that closing yourself off to loving something or someone is no way to live, and we can weather the worst of hurts for there is strength found in our vulnerability. You learn that life goes on and is achingly beautiful, and you appreciate those aches and beauty in a way you never could before.

I like to think that Dog's soul will go on somewhere beyond here. That he will have his own rebirth. Perhaps he will go to a place unseen, where he plays with other Dogs who served faithfully as best friends and wait for the day I join him. Perhaps I will encounter his spirit again when I am ready to bring a new furry companion into my life.

Perhaps his sweet, little essence will continue to hover protectively over me in the world behind the veil, and though I can't see him, I will sense that he will always be out there keeping watch. Many people might tell me these are fanciful thoughts, and maybe they are, but to them I would say—

If you think me fanciful, you have obviously not known the love of an Old Dog.

88

II. After Dog

The house is so quiet tonight. Empty. It wasn't supposed to happen like this. So sudden.

*H*e was my Best Friend. My Ever Present. My Boon Companion. We just celebrated his 15th birthday a few days ago, yet he told me today, unequivocally, it was time say goodbye. I am grateful for that. Grateful that he took care of me up until the end and let me know, "Mom, it's time. Now."

Sometimes you have to learn to let go.

I have no questions that I made the right decision. His gaze this morning said it all. And though tonight it is hard to breathe, we had an almost perfect last night and day. Bedtime stories. I held him for the entire night. Carried him around the duck pond and rose garden in the morning, because he wasn't able to walk. Took him to his favorite places around town. Went for a drive. Gave him a last biscuit. Said goodbye to our home and the office. Licked one last client with care.

We reminisced; I told him exactly who he has been to me and how fast my heart beats for him, but he already knew all of that, I just needed to say it for me. Told him he was the best of the best of the best. Thanked him for loving me so long and so hard for so many years.

Then I told him goodbye. It was okay to let go. It was okay to release me.

Because that's what Love does.

It lets go.

I have no doubt he would still be sitting in my lap right now. Hurting, suffering, hanging on if I hadn't told him it was okay to go. Once I said the words—he needed to hear them, was waiting for my blessing—he began to release. They are some of the hardest words I have spoken, but I figure any being who was brave enough to be present and love me in my life, deserves for me to be present and love him through his death.

For years he tended me so carefully, I was his flock of one. Today was my time to tend him. And even though I didn't want to let go, to feel the pain of loss, the empty gaps that are now gaping, I knew that trying to hang on and will him to stay isn't love: it's a cage, made of invisible bars of force and expectation. I often don't understand Life, but I do understand Love. It is not about hanging on, it is about releasing, allowing, and letting go.

To love somebody is to offer them up for the freeing. Again and again and again.

And now Dog is Free.

I do not know what comes After Dog. They say Life will go on, but for tonight, for tonight it stops. I allow myself to be directionless, lost, heartbroken. And grateful. So very grateful that I should know such unconditional love. That I should have the moments I did. That I should know exactly what it is to have one's heart filled without regard to genus and species and with total regard to the amount of love one holds.

And Dog, well he had a lot of Love in his heart. The best of the best of the best.

89

III. A Kintsugi Pup for My Kintsugi Heart

for Corrie, who said he was perfect, thank you—for all the things

I got a new pup today. I call him Kintsugi Pup. For my Kintsugi Heart.

Kintsugi: A Japanese tradition of repairing broken pottery bowls by filling in the cracks with gold. It is thought that over time the bowl becomes more lovely as its flaws are mended with this brilliant liquid, creating a beautiful piece of imperfect perfection out of something that was in shards. The art of Kintsugi doesn't aim to hide that which was shattered but to illuminate the damage, with the knowledge that at the end of the process the piece will become more magnificent than it was before.

One need not stretch out and reach too far before grasping the beautiful metaphor Kintsugi holds for the condition of the human heart, for the beautiful heart does not come from that which has never broken, but that which has cracked and fallen to pieces. It is those moments of brokenness that create space for light to shine through, so we can make room for more love.

I made room for more love today in the form of a new friend. A tiny harbinger of love wrapped in a ball of fluff. It was sort of unexpected, yet it was only a matter of time before a furry sidekick made their way into my life; I am definitely a girl who needs a dog.

I had my eye on another guy all week, even applied for adoption, because I was convinced he was *my guy*. I woke up this morning to a rather crushing email saying somebody else already adopted him, I guess he wasn't *my guy* after all. Then I had a plan B, another pup I had been eying. She had some issues with men after being a backyard breeding dog and was a bit shy according to her profile. This seemed to cause concern among people close to me: *She sounds too challenging, maybe she has too many behavioral issues, you don't want that!*

I had a rough reaction to all the feedback; it hit me in my most wounded places where I am still letting the light enter, so I pathetically laid in Dog's tiny bed dolefully sobbing. I bawled for many reasons.

1) I miss my best friend. I am trying to open my heart to a new friend, because I think it is better to share love than hold onto grief, but I didn't realize adoption would be so hard when I'm in such a fragile space. I didn't expect to get my hopes up and watch them tumble.

2) I realize I am not in the best space to do a giant search on every rescue site for the "perfect" dog. I'm not sure what that even means, and I certainly don't have the energy for it. Dog wasn't perfect, he was a ripe mess when I first got him. It was our imperfect love that really made things perfect in the end.

3) And underneath all those excellent surface reasons, in my heart of hearts, I keep thinking, *but I could be this dog.*

I have been used and hurt, quite badly at times, by men. Some days it still takes a lot for me to self organize and allow masculine presence into my life. Sometimes I feel scared too, and I want to run away. I'm pushing myself to move past all that and keep reminding myself to keep my heart open, but sometimes I wonder (and half expect)—what if I have too many behavioral issues and am not wanted? Like they don't want her? Because she is not a clean, shiny bowl anymore? I can relate to this wounded dog. I too have similar wounds in need of more gold.

As I lay crying in Dog's old bed, life feels like too much. I decide to skip the adoption clinic, something I had proactively decided I would go to earlier in the week when I was sure I would get Dog A, and if not that, have a backup plan for Dog B. But after laying on an tattered, fuzzy blanket that still smells so sweetly like my best friend, I can feel myself closing to life.

Too much, too hard, too soon, I think. Let's put this new dog thing on hold for awhile, maybe forever. I can't handle the expectation, pressure, and mirror of self this process is holding up to the cracks in my foundation. I had just made up my mind and then a friend of my heart, who knows I am a better BethAnne with a dog, convinced me otherwise: *What can it hurt? I'll go with you.*

I walk in and see one small pup. White with a black spot. Crazy, patchy hair. In desperate need of a bath. Wicked under bite. Sharp brown eyes. I hold him as they tell me he has been with them for many months after his previous owners gave him away, because they were elderly and his energy surpassed their capacities.

Since then he has been at the rescue, mostly in a kennel. Nobody wants him even though he's small, well behaved, and sweet as can be. They tell me everybody thinks he's ugly, that some people find him odd and strange looking. They want handsome dogs. Pretty dogs. Uncracked bowls. Perfect pieces I suppose.

He stays in my arms a long time. They tell me it is the longest anybody has bothered to hold him. My friend says, *he's perfect*, and I can't disagree. He seems pretty comfortable, then he presses his head against my chest the same way Dog always did—Dog was weird and strange looking too. So I decide I should keep holding him as long as I possibly can, as I tell him we understand weird and odd around these parts.

And now we find ourselves stealing glances at one another while I write these words, both of us a little uncertain as to how to proceed, both of us now stuck with one another, both of us wondering who each other is.

The love of any dog is liquid gold, made only of the finest stuff, here to remind us what the word *unconditional* means. Dog taught me that, giving me pure love which wove itself through my flaws with gleaming care, and as I contemplate my new friend and what lessons he has to teach me, I thoughtfully consider my Kintsugi Heart. I have a feeling if you could take it out for a look, you would see a lot of gold throughout.

There are a multitude of stories among the golden seams; the last few years have not been kind to keeping my heart intact, and there is much in me that has felt flawed and broken. Yet I've continued to learn that the beautiful thing about life and love is that if one keeps their heart open and finds the courage to stare their flaws in the face and embrace them with compassion, they will eventually find liquid gold. They will come face to face with just how Enough they are.

I may have pieces that broke, but that breaking is precisely what allowed Light to enter, and it is the act of delving into the cracks and fissures, bringing illumination to what feels broken and dark, which creates a beautiful whole.

Our lives: they can become these gorgeous bowls of broken ceramic, mended with gold again and again, if one has the audacity to remain vulnerable and allow the breaking. If one has the boldness to know that healing means staying your course, diving into the pain, finding beauty among the ashes, facing your flaws head on and saying: *I see you. You are loved. I am loved. All of me.*

The night is still. My new friend is curled into a ball on a blanket staring at me with a curious, open gaze: I can't wait for the two of us to get to know each other. I stare back at this scraggly, snaggle tooth creature I've invited into heart and home; something good has happened here today.

A Kintsugi Pup for my Kintsugi Heart.

90

IV. The Love Inside

I'm in Oregon surrounded by gray mist and red tinged trees thinking of how a year ago today, I also found myself in this beautiful state. I was here to race Silver Falls Marathon and having just lost my beloved Dog the week before, I arrived feeling like a bedraggled orphan seeking sanctuary from the onslaught of grief that had haunted me all week.

*M*y life was knocked out of gravitational orbit. I felt no sense of affiliation or family with him gone. I was unanchored, and I had never felt more lost. I had a dull hope that somewhere among the pine laden trails and warmth of friendship that had invited me to the lovely state, I'd find something healing in the journey.

I remember sitting in a coffee shop that first day with my writing and art supplies, seeking refuge in the comfort of creativity and forcing myself to post a picture of a bright red tree on my Facebook page. I didn't want to post that picture at first, because I had only been posting about Dog. Talking and writing about him was keeping him alive inside of me somehow. Posting something other than him meant life was moving on.

I didn't want life to move on. I wanted things the way they were. Every step away from how it had been was a step towards something new, foreign, and highly uncomfortable. That bright red tree represented more than just fall beauty and sharing my trip to Oregon on social media, it was the beginning of my acceptance of change.

I felt that same resistance in me this last weekend as I went through the one year anniversary of Dog's loss, and realized how deeply the imprint of sorrow and felt sense of experience is still imbedded in my cellular structure. I was completely unprepared for the heavy tears that came of their own accord throughout the week or the ache which dulled my tired heart.

It is amazing how strongly we store information in our bodies. It was almost as if anything that didn't get expressed last year was determined to have its say and simply waited patiently for the right time to release. I felt like I was losing him all over again, and I couldn't figure out why it was so potent. It dawned on me that similar to posting that picture of the bright red tree last October, my reluctant admission life was moving on, I was struggling a year later with admitting how much life has moved on.

The memories of my beloved Dog and our tiny simple life together are still so fresh and alive. Always one to use fall as a time for introspection and reflection on the passage of time from a year earlier, I remember much of last fall and all the memories that include him. They make me smile. They make him feel close to my heart.

Next fall will be different. There will be new memories when I reflect back. This Oregon trip will lay fresher in my mind than last time. The imprints of this fall will be more easily accessible than a year ago.

Life is changing, and while I believe I will always remember Dog's life with me, it will be further away on the timeline than it is now. My memories are going to fade, replaced by new ones, and my awareness of this truth makes me feel I am losing something dear to me.

It is profoundly beautiful how deeply humans hang on to that which they have loved. How difficult it is for us to release the reigns back to life, acknowledge that life is moving on, admit that we don't know what the future holds. That the future is always an unwritten possibility. New. Foreign. Highly uncomfortable. That it is okay to feel lost until we find our way again.

Here is what I do know. Last year I sat blogging at an outside table as sunshine streamed down and yellow leaves swirled merrily, and I realized something so simple it seemed silly to write. Yet it went so deep I could feel the healing my heart craved: *The love inside, we take it with us.* It will always live on. Beyond bodies, beyond circumstances, beyond timelines, beyond change. Love is greater than death, and so it can never be taken from us. Even when those we've loved have gone on.

I felt this truth settling into me as I sipped apple cider and watched the golden leaves dance, and I realized the love I had for him hadn't changed with his passing. In fact, it felt even stronger, because I loved beyond the physical realm. It would never be changed by time, space, or distance. It may now exist only in my heart without an object to bestow it upon, but it is as real as real can be. Surely to love like that is one of the greatest gifts one can ever receive.

I wrap myself in that knowledge. Place it upon my shoulders like a mantle of strength and take it with me wherever I go. I feel powerful in my ability to love so steadfast and blessed with grace that I can feel that love humming happily in my heart, realizing that somewhere under the layers of sadness lays something so pure and beautiful.

And now it is a year later, and I'm cozily ensconced on a sofa staring out at a rainy day ripe with autumn colors, and I am realizing this lesson all over again. The new loves in our lives do not take away from that which was there before. They only add to it. Making it stronger and more beautiful.

Memories may fade, and it's true that every step forward is a step away, but we are not here to stay in the same place. We are here to venture into the new, foreign, and uncomfortable. We are here to learn about love. And learning about love requires great courage to face the come what mays. It requires loss. It requires the admission things have changed. It requires letting go of what was, so we can make room for who and what we'll be.

That's okay though, because in the end, we will never lose what matters most. It will always live on. Through pine laden trails, and bright red trees, and misty changing landscapes, and new loves, and new experiences, and new characters in our scripts. Wherever we go, we take it with us—

The Love inside.

91

WE WILL HAVE JOY

There are going to be days when despite our best efforts, we just can't connect to that which is good. And that's okay. Especially when suffering and processing loss, it is important to know the scope of the darkness, so we can learn to find the stars that guide our way.

*B*ut when it is time and those stars have led us through the worst of it, we have to make a choice about how we choose to see this life and what we choose to nurture inside of us. And if we want to find what is beautiful in this world, then one has to be rather persistent when it comes to joy and gratitude. These gifts can quietly start to dissolve when we are not actively tending to them, a slow continental drift that leaves us with only tiny shards of good.

Every day we are given a choice. Life asks us a question: *Who do you want to be in this world?*

The way we choose to live is our response.

Our perspectives, attitudes, thoughts, heart energy—that's all on us. Nothing external can change that. Change is an inside job. We are the ones who have to insist on finding joy. Even when life has handed us a heap of gritty muck, at some point, we have to choose to find the gifts anyways. To see there is always space for new ideas, new moments, new intentions, new loves, new letting goes, new skies, new experiences, new interactions, new beginnings, new moons, new creations, new imaginings, new places.

New heart spaces.

All just waiting for us to recognize them, grab onto them, and shape them according to our energy, efforts, and intents so we can choose to find the gifts of their day. The gifts that increase joy, love, happiness, and gratitude. Some days we just have to work a little harder for it, but we all have the capacity inside of ourselves to do the work. To change our set points. To challenge ourselves to be more than our circumstances.

To insist that in this moment, on this day, no matter where we find ourselves—we will have joy.

92

So much loss and so much life
all intermingled into one.

Each one birthing the other in a never ending ouroboros of love
and mystery:

Our losses making life that much more sacred,
the sacred infusing our losses with life.

93

HOME

We cannot return to innocence once we've passed the threshold of loss, but we can return to ourselves. We can reach up and stretch out and dig deep and do whatever we need to do in order to excavate our own sense of self and find a home there, within our hearts.

here is one task on this earth each of us is better able to do than anybody else, and that is to try and be our most unequivocal, authentic, true blue self. Even in grief, we can do this by finding ways to honor our losses that feel authentic, real, and loving to the whole of who we are.

There is much in this world that will break us. Shatter us into shards, make us aware of parts of ourselves we never knew existed, turn a light on in our darkened rooms so we can see the full scope of who we are. Even in this darkness, we can learn to embody what it is to be real.

Loss can break. Life can break. Our hearts can break. Our tears can fall. We can remend and repair and rewire and reinvent, only to find Life comes along and breaks us all over again. But there is a fundamental wellness in our souls that goes unharmed. It is called Love, and no matter how often our pieces break, they will reform themselves around that core again and again.

Some things cannot be broken, and so long as you hold Love in your heart—no matter how far you wander off the path—you will always find your way home.

94

EXODUS

It's pouring rain and the geese are making a racket outside, probably discussing preparations for their annual fall exodus. It may only be late August, but the sunshine and blooms of June and July blinked and here we find ourselves in Alaska's rainy season, the cusp of summer into fall, where there are clean scents of cool in the breeze, the beginning turn of the leaves, and a sun that is taking much longer to rise.

*E*verything is changing, myself along with it. Part of me wants to flee with those geese in mass migration. After the claustrophobic grief of last winter, I cringe at thinking of plunging into another season of darkness. But a bigger part is ready to immerse myself in the change, knowing this season will be different; it's our last winter here, a finality that makes everything seem more cherished and heightened when you realize you will not experience these moments again. And it's the latter part who has spent her summer reveling in the change, contemplating how sacred and precious each and every day is.

We live life sometimes like we are waiting for something big to happen, waiting for those moments that make it all seem worth it. But lately, I am realizing that every moment is the moment that tells us it's all worth it. That life is a gift, and even on dreary, gray days like today, it is a privilege to feel and breathe and be, to embody what it means to be so human.

It is the All of our experience, the Full, that makes us who we are. Not just the big moments.

Having said that, there are big moments coming up, our move to Kauai perhaps the biggest one of all. It has taken a great deal of courage to get to a place of recognition that if I want to ungroove myself from the deep ruts that feel like life in Anchorage, I am going to have to manifest that change and trust Life to support me in the process.

We often forget that Life isn't happening to us. That instead, we are in a relationship with Life, and as such, Life sometimes sits and waits, giving us free reign to make choices, preparing to meet us and work with us when and where those choices are made. The steps we take in our tomorrows created by the decisions we make in our todays.

In February of 2015, my husband and I were vacationing in Kauai, and we made the decision to move there someday. It was more than just a "paradise is so nice we never want to leave" kind of whim, but a decision rooted deeply in a felt sense that Life had something planned for us on that island. We both sprang to life there. He like a plant, withering in the dark of Alaska, coming back to life, growing big and strong in the heart of the sun. Me like one of the island's tropical flowers who felt a sense of fruition and bloom and greater color in the magic of that place.

Kauai is rich with life, and with a yearning to pour life into the world with my creativity, writing, and art, I can't think of a better place to support that process. Or to cradle our family in sunshine and warmth as we start new and build a home together.

Then we came back from vacation with these good intents and fell back into the pattern of daily life. Our 3 year plan turned into 5 years turned into 7 years. The responsibility and security of my private practice seemed like too much to give up, our newly purchased home an anchor to hold us to this space, the familiarity of this town easy. Convenient.

Then last winter came and both of us suffered the dark so severely in December the move date started shifting back to sooner rather than later in our minds. Then after Brent, I started to wonder what I was doing with my life. Why I was trading security for my dreams. Why I was living out of alignment with the truth of what I feel called to do.

So we decided next spring is when it is. Even with all the unknowns and uncertainties and details of how it's going to happen, it will happen. A prospect that is terrifying and exhilarating and absolutely feels right. And now that our intent is set and plans are being made, part of trusting the process is seeing how Life will meet us in the process and carve out a way.

Though there is a great deal before us that feels daunting, what felt impossible a year ago now feels realizable. The intentions and decisions we are laying down today, paving the way for a new tomorrow. We are our own powerful agents of change when we let ourselves be.

In the meantime, the rain is falling; and I am cramming in all the Alaskan experiences I can; and we camped by a waterfall last weekend—absolute magic; and books are beginning to spin out of me when I have the time to weave; and I cried the other night when I realized that if I make it to 80, I will have spent half of my life without my brother; and the full moon is beginning to wane; and the geese are still nattering in exodus; and there are candles burning bright as I write, warming the chill that has come with this morn; and it is a privilege to feel and breathe and be on this tired Tuesday, to embody what it means to be so human.

And it is the All of our experience, the Full, that makes us who we are.

95

ACHE

Some days I still miss him terribly. I don't know when those days will come, they just sort of creep up and grab you. An unexpected visitation of the past.

And it's on those days, where the emptiness inside feels so profound, you can't help but feel the ache in the place *they* once filled.

I sense that ache, and I realize it will never go away, nor was it meant to. That yes, there will be times—many, many good times as life goes about the business of carrying on—where I'm not aware of its presence, but there will be other times where all I'm reminded of is what I have lost.

And on those days, I am simply learning to tilt my face to the sky, let the wind whisper in my ear telling me he's all right, and recognize the ache for what it is:

A song of love in a wanting space.

96

BALLOONS

As much as I'd like to be like the proverbial girl in the picture about to release the last of her balloons, I have never found release to be this easy.

*L*etting go of something doesn't take place in one fell swoop or a single instance. It happens in small bits and pieces; the time you cried it out over there, the time you sat with your sad over here. It happens in the quiet of your waking hours, and it happens in the deep of your subconscious as you sleep.

It happens as you take brave steps forward, and it happens as you create new memories to add to your timeline that help soften the distance between the immediacy of the things you're trying to release. It happens in giant bursts and small drops and all the in betweens where you find yourself just trying to do the work of living life.

Letting go is a process and not an immediate one. We are best served by releasing all expectations of time constraints on when we should let go. Twenty-five years might pass and your heart will still ache in that same spot reminding you how great the magnitude of consequence that occupied that place. So hold those balloons for as long as you need and only release when you know good and well it is time.

We'll let go when we let go, and only if it's right for our heart. There are some things we're meant to keep forever, some loves that run so deep they are eternally bound.

97

HOPE

There are two ways we can go through life: with hope or without hope.

And I figure it's just a bit easier to make our way along this crazy, winding path with hope as a companion. I know sometimes it seems hard to find, but it's really very simple. The clouds may part and the light shines down, and you've been told to keep the faith. A bird flies across your path singing along, and you've been reminded to find joy. The sky changes in tone and shade and you remember so it is with life; no season lasts forever. Outside of us, or within us.

Our realities can be marked by dream or despair, and they become what we choose to make of them. It is a choice of perspective that lays in the eyes of the one doing the perceiving.

As for me, I decided long ago this world already has too much that has abandoned hope in place of despondency, and I will make no further contributions to that. As long as I am given a choice as to who I keep for companions, I will choose to walk through this world with a perspective of belief and the glow of hope by my side.

98

Dancing Leaves

Any undoing, any shedding, any losing creates a space where life has room to pour new things into us.

$\mathcal{E}$ ndings are a genesis for potential. Metamorphosis happens in the void when we have to find a way through the darkness. It is the metaphorical space where the caterpillar reaches the end of his world and becomes a butterfly: desperation providing the ingredients for inspiration, chaos the material for creation. The space where the leaf learns to free itself by falling from the tree, returning to the ground so it can become the soil and seed for new life.

It can feel like a terrible thing when life brings us to the end of the world as we know it, to the end of something inside ourselves. When we can't see anything but black space beyond our current space, and we are left to trust that if we go forward, relinquish control, and have faith in the process we will discover our chrysalis.

We all have our own paths to this precipice of change. We arrive through loss of relationship, through hardship and difficulty, through illness and injury. Through the end of a chapter we sometimes realize we were done writing long before we set down the pen. At times we are deposited here unceremoniously when we suddenly lose something we never believed we would lose, and we find ourselves at the mercy of Life's forces.

We are brought here so we can choose whether to contract in fear, trying to squeeze ourselves back into an old shell of self that no longer fits, or to expand in faith, venturing into the black space of the unknown, believing we will find new ground if we are brave enough to see the journey through.

The journey requires a great deal of surrender, for it is only in letting go of how we think things should be, that we can develop into who we are meant to be: a never ending cycle of dancing leaves who learn to grow when it is time to grow and when to drop when Life calls us to release. We are undone, so we can become.

99

IF YOU STRIKE ME DOWN

What if love just grows more powerful when someone leaves us?

*I*f that love is good and pure and true, what if removing the shells of a body and the physical act of being in each other's presence, well, what if it removes that which is material in love and simply leaves us with that which is divine?

What if Love somehow grows stronger after? What if there is more to come? What if there are lessons for our hearts that we haven't yet imagined, because that particular spiritual and emotional shell had yet to be broken prior to our loss? What if those we love are still out there teaching us, guiding us, helping us, and the act of learning to let go holds more significance than we grasp?

What if Obi-Wan had it right all along when he said, "If you strike me down, I shall become more powerful than you can possibly imagine." What if the power of Love just gets stronger after, and the act of release and surrender become the ingredients we need to grow and ascend and make space in our heart for more Love?

What if when you take away all the physical manifestations, and the love still lives on and we still hang onto the essence of love for who and what we've lost, what if it is us who become more powerful than we possibly imagined?

Then we are not just those who have loved and lost, but we become these beautiful, powerful beings who find a way to transform and transcend the dark of pain by finding the courage to see our love for what it is: an expression of divinity shining out in the darkness, reminding us no matter how much pain it holds, there are still forces in this world capable of magic, mystery, and light.

100

ALWAYS

But I don't want to lose you, she said.
He smiled so sweet and spoke, eyes kind:

You cannot lose me.
It is impossible.

I am the part of your heart
which remembered what you always knew,
yet thought you forgot,
LOVE.

I am in you as you are in me.
So you see, losing me would be losing you.

Now point your compass due North.
Look to the stars when all seems dark.
Keep your heart true and remember:

You cannot lose what your heart already found.
You cannot lose love.
It lasts for always.

101

SATELLITES

I sold my old, faithful Jetta this week. Silver, square, a so-called sport wagon, which falls uncomfortably close to the station wagon category, it's carried me many miles. On road and in life.

A round town, up to mountains, out on adventures, towards lakes and trails and trees; away from a cookie cutter, inauthentic self and down a quirky, wild, unmapped road of the heart. That car has seen me through a great deal.

I have to admit I shed a few tears after it was gone, even felt bad for the little car, like it would think I abandoned it and didn't want it anymore. But it was time. I'm driving my brother's Durango now, Dad had it all fixed up and put some wicked all terrain tires on for back road adventuring—we would never have spent last weekend camping by a giant waterfall if not for that beast—and I just don't need two cars.

Still though, I have felt the loss of the vehicle that represented so many growing pains and becomings, along with a growing awareness of just how much stuff we are going to have to release before we move.

Letting go is definitely not for the faint of heart. I don't think we realize the emotional, energetic and physical space that objects and people take up in our lives. The towns we live, the homes we inhabit, the people we call family and friends, the things that fill our homes, the wheels that take us from one place to another—it's like we're all teeny, tiny satellites who learn to gravitate towards and orbit around the planets of our personal solar systems based on all the other teeny, tiny satellites in the area.

We arrange our lives around all the things that fill our space.

Then something shifts and depending on how big that something is, you get knocked out of orbit. At best, it's a small shift and you can quickly adapt, find your way back on course again. But sometimes the shift is so profound you get knocked out of the system entirely.

I drove that Jetta away from an old life once, the trunk packed with clothes and books and boxes of sadness. Backed out of a house for the last time, a place I was never again going to call home. Drove down the road to a new address, about 300 square feet in the bottom of somebody else's home where I paid rent and painted the walls light blue. Strewn with twinkling white lights, bright pictures, and jars of flowers, I began to learn that I had needed to travel outside of my old lines and go beyond the boundaries of my former self, so I could find out who I truly was meant to be in this life.

Spinning and disoriented, I was knocked out of my old system entirely. I no longer had a physical home or a partner in life who created a sense of home. I had to learn how to build a home inside my heart, so I could take that sense of belonging with me everywhere I went. I found myself zooming around in my trusty sport wagon to the different satellites that began to compose the new landscape of my life. New faces, new spaces, new places: that faithful car helped me find new orbit.

I learned a lot about letting go in those years. That it can break your heart. That the heart is a remarkably resilient creature. That anytime we willingly release and clear out an old space, life will always bring us to a new space of self. That life will honor our leaps of faith when we are called to jump. That you can't negotiate with life and keep one foot on the security of shore if you want to see what's waiting on the other side.

Those were the years where a handful of men came and went— some of them quite crushing—and I learned even more about the necessity of boundaries, and goodbyes, and how the heart has the capacity to knit itself back together and find a way to keep expanding when we learn to love ourselves. Those were the years my old gremlin, ever present, constant companion, who I affectionately called Dog, passed away—and I learned that the love we have inside will always be with us, that love endures beyond the physicality of this place.

And those were the years I finally found new love on a rainy, Oregonian, serendipitous day. Which eventually led me to expand my sense of home to include one former Oregonian, two little white dogs, one temperamental calico cat, and a small cottage in the woods with rainbow walls and secret gardens. Like I said earlier, anytime we willingly release and clear out an old space, life will always bring us to a new space of self. I've loved this current space, but I'm being called to go again, leave this solar system behind.

Death will change you; Brent's death changed me. Pushed me to go sooner rather than later. I'm scared sometimes. Overwhelmed at others. Totally rip roaring excited underneath it all. Ready to see how Life shows up for this leap of faith. And ready, though difficult it will be, to let go when it is time to let go.

That little, silver bullet is part of the past, and is now carting his new owner around, making new Alaskan memories. While I have palm trees in my—not quite so distant as it felt back in the spring/getting scarily close—future. And a Durango with wicked all terrain tires that's going with me, capable of driving out on the white sandy beaches of my brother's favorite beach, MacArthur Park.

We'll pop the trunk, let a couple little white dogs run free. Stare out at the ocean, say *hello* to the other side. Bask in the sun, be for a bit. Then head back to a new space of home.

102

WINGS

for Liz

What a brief beat—
Life.

We think it's forever
and then it's not,
and we are left
wondering
if we did what
we came here
to do.

In the end,
it's not about the
accomplishments,
achievements,
the things we did:

It's just about the
Love.

How we loved.
And why we loved.
And when and if we loved—
when Life gave
us an Open,
every time we sensed
a Close.

My god, I know it hurts—
my dear, sweet, girl.
To cradle this loss

within your arms,
and lay your love
to grave.

I cannot take it
from you,
but I can tell you—
from the travails
of experience:

You can shrink
or you can grow.
You will contract
and then expand.
And just when
you think it's over...

When you've wandered
off the cliff
into a scape of waste,
from which you can't
bounce back,

My dear girl,
you will learn to fly—

Take your loss
into your heart
and let yourself
be
so much more
than before ...

Until you are this
magical creature
who soars through the night—

With knowing wings
of Elysian.

103

Creatures of the Deep

A few years ago I stopped asking why.

here are a lot of whys in this world, such is Life. We live in a beautiful world, but there are rips and tears in its fabric that any of us can get caught in. And of course when you get snagged, have it out with Life if you need. Have it out with your Higher Self. Have it out with The Universe. Have it out with the Forces That Be. Have it out with God and the Fates and the Destinies and the What Could Have Beens.

Have it out as much as you need for as long as you need. Just know that for some things the question of *why?* will only take you down a dead end road that leads to little except resentment, bitterness, and self-pity. And if this is where you need to be for a bit to experience these emotions, then, by all means, be where you need to be. We deserve to feel what we feel—and sometimes need to feel it long and fast and hard—before we are ready to move on and feel other things.

But at some point—for our own wellness, our own healing, our own moving through and mending of hearts—I have found it helpful to accept that Life happens. Stuff happens. Things will come to pass in this place. Sometimes it's wonderful and good. Sometimes it's tragic and sad. And a better question than *why?* is the question of how we choose to navigate it.

Do we do something destructive or choose to construct something new?

Do we stay open to life or close ourselves off to the world?

Do we remain in the broken place of what was or try and move into the space of what may be?

We don't have a say about the things that break us, we can only say what we'll do with our pieces. And no matter how fractured and shattered those pieces may be, we are all equipped with the glue of love—each of us finding it in our own ways, in our own forms. And it is up to us to find a way to mend those pieces back together.

Make them into something more nuanced than they were before. Bigger. Deeper. More authentic. So we can keep growing into these beautiful, numinous creatures of the deep, who always figure out a way, even in the dark, to find the light.

104

Eclipse

Grief will bring you to an eclipse of the soul. It is where you will find your darkest hours and know your darkest nights. But my friend, please know that any good dark night of the soul is a possible gateway to light.

This is the space where you will begin to discover your truth. Where everything else is burned away except that which is meant to matter. Where clarity becomes a companion and these bones of humanity the place where you learn just how deep and far and wide love can stretch.

We have this illusion in this life that we are somehow separated from Love. That it is outside of us and something we need to seek out, grasp for, cling to. But the truth is, *that* is only an illusion: Love has been within us all along. We just had to make space to find it.

And if you have dared to stare grief in the face and make the passage of dark back to the hope of light, discovered new strength to carry on, scratched your way out of the shadows, found the sacred rhythm beating through the veins of these times which allows this world to keep on spinning, then you know grief for exactly what it is.

The hardest, most powerful teacher on Love we have ever had.

105

FROM THE GROUND UP

I think perhaps October
is the most beautiful,
yet saddest, month of all.

Her face drip leaven tears,
soaking the ground with her loss.

The more she tries to grasp,
to save, to hang on,
the harder they fall.

She doesn't yet realize
she is watering her own roots.
Strengthening, lengthening, nourishing
the space she inhabits
so she can rise up and
be bigger, be taller,
bloom anew.

Then fall in love with Life,
fall in love with Herself,
fall in love with Love
all over again.

From the
ground
up.

106

OCTOBER SKY

The sun rose carelessly over the mountains this morning, a pomegranate orb of life bathing the day with soft amber and plum light. It's beginning to take long enough to rise that I am reminded October is here, and we are on the cusp of that time of year where we rapidly lose our light as we approach the dark of Winter Solstice, where light becomes almost an afterthought of grace, and the dark is where we must learn to find joy.

*B*ut for now it is still fall, and I decided that October is an auspicious month—where the leaves find the pristine courage to turn and let go—to do a little more letting go of my own. I've been doing a lot of clearing of space lately, and I found a few things that need to be released before I leave this state.

This week I realized I still have Dog's ashes, and as he was my Best Friend *here*—in Alaska, I believe they should be laid to rest where our love resided. I also found a small box that needed to be laid to rest alongside. Its contents are only tiny scraps of paper, nothing that would seem important to anybody else if they opened it; they represent the ashes of the world I once lived and the lessons learned there.

It was June 2014, and my boyfriend (soon to be fiancée soon to be husband) was making the move from Bend, Oregon to Alaska after 6 months of long distance dating. I knew I was about to cross through a threshold of change upon his arrival. This was never a "let's try this out for awhile, take it slow" kind of deal, it was a "Love or Bust" situation. He moved into my 300 square foot space, we bought a house not long after, and we dove into each other and love and figuring out couplehood all at the same time.

I curled up in bed by myself for the last time the night before his arrival in a sea of surreality and an awareness: *it is all going to change on the morrow.* Though I am excited and ready for this new chapter, I am bittersweet knowing the chapter of being just me—of being my single self, of learning all the beautiful and painful and heart expanding lessons I have learned in the wake of my divorce—is at an end.

So I take a beautiful box, a small tin with a brilliant gold sun on the front, and I write down all the gifts I learned in that space in time. Words like, "I learned to carry the full of who I am," "I learned how to love myself," "I learned to embrace my light side and my shadow side," "I learned what it is to unconditionally LOVE from Dog," "I learned how strong I am," "I learned how to write my truth," "I learned to claim the space of myself," and "I learned how to be still and listen," soon fill the box.

I mean to bury that box in the ground soon after. Let the words be nourished by the earth. Lay to rest this beautiful shell of a younger self who held me so hard and so well. Let the burying be a symbol of release that represents my willingness to choose new space to grow. Then time did what it always does and slips on past, so I never do.

This week I found that box along with Dog's ashes, and I decided, since he is such an integral part of my heart, so intertwined with all those beautiful lessons, to return them to earth together. To lay him and my younger self to rest under an October sky in the chocolates and mulberries and mahoganies of the ground.

It is a simple occasion. I take the tins to a favorite wooded trail, dig up a little earth, and place them beneath the watchful gaze of a wise old tree who feels welcoming and warm. Nothing particularly remarkable happens, but then again all that is remarkable from Dog and my younger self and the lessons of those days is now carried deep inside of me. I have buried these boxes to represent the shedding of old shells, and that's the thing about old shells—they don't house new life.

It's calm and cold, but the sun brings life and light, so I go sit on a nearby bench that greets me like an old friend. It's not my first time on that bench, and I stay there for quite awhile beneath the gaze of a blue soaked sky remembering.

Remembering the times I sat on that bench with Dog. Remembering the times I sat on that bench and learned to talk to the sky and the trees and the world around and within me, learned that as long as I have a relationship with Life, I will never be lonely.

Remembering the times my brother and I took Dog for a walk there—Brent loved him fiercely, was with me the day he died, considered himself part owner—through the trails in the woods on soft spring nights. Remembering the times of who I was: the girl who wrote those heart lessons out on tiny scraps of papers, thanked her teachers of yesterday, and placed them in a tin box with exquisite hope in her heart for her future.

I say farewell to all that has come to pass. *Auf Wiedersehen* and *Thank You* to all that was and no longer is. *Ashes to ashes and dust to dust and love to love*; I release what I can in that moment to the clouds and the sun and the great space of sky. I walk away, one last glance at the earth, a nod and acknowledgment of what lays buried beneath, and I ask the land to keep it safe.

Goodbye, goodbye, goodbye, I say.

I choose new space.

The land hears my release. Somewhere across a distant ocean she sends a song on a bright, tropical breeze and answers back with the warmest of welcome.

Hello. Hello. Hello.

107

ALL THAT IS SHABBY AND BRIGHT

Loss will take you to the core of what it means to be human. Like the cycle of the seasons, who teach us how to release and return and rebirth and reclaim, it is okay to be full and complete in this task.

*R*emembering that is so hard for us at times. We expect ourselves to entertain life with our best foot forward and a sense that we have it together. We place expectations and judgments on how we think we should be handling things. We feel to be messy and vulnerable and chaotic is to fail at this misdirected, self-appointed task.

But loss is completely chaotic. Undeniably vulnerable. Sloppy and disheveled. And achingly untidy.

Our emotions do not turn off when something is over, as if relationships are a linear process. We cannot expect something to end and expect our hearts to accordingly end all emotional attachment as well, like we can simply dispose of those emotions and move forward to what's next. And if something ends because of death, which is the most final ending of all, then we can expect to take all the emotions that come from heartbreak and times that by the thousands.

Whoever they have been to us—those who've touched us in a profound way, those we intertwined ourselves with on a deeper level, those who left our lives leaving scrapes and holes and pangs in our hearts—they will never be disposable. There will always be traces of someone who left a footprint in our internal gardens.

Our responsibility to ourselves isn't to deny that these imprints exist, but to make space for those who've impacted our lives, to make space for those we've loved and lost. Our responsibility is to honor the mess of our response and know there is room for all of our feelings. Our responsibility is to remember our relationship to grief isn't linear: it is fluid.

Circular, cyclical, seasonal, full. Subject to movement and change, as it continues to seek healing that waters and weeds and grows and warms our gardens to wellness. Our responsibility to ourselves is to learn to love ourselves wherever we are at and simply accept that this too—all that is shabby and all that is bright—is what it means to be human.

108

HONOR THEM

There is no right or wrong way to grieve. To process our losses. To remember those who've passed in this place. There are some signatures written so strongly inside of us they will forever remain engraved. Years may go by, and you may still feel the ache and the love in the place they hold inside your being.

This is the cost of loving and losing. To feel that love and ache and realize there is nobody else who will carry that experience, carry their remembrance, carry that love inside of you in the unique way you do. And since you are the keeper of this very precious task, you should not be afraid to remember and honor them any way you see fit, whenever you see fit.

Make up your own rituals of remembrance. Throw flowers in the river in release. Write letters and burn them in a fire, let the smoke and ash curl up towards the sky and reach the ears of those you love. Light candles of intention and memory. Surround yourself with pictures or prized possessions. Name a star after them. Talk to them daily. Talk to them in the moon, in your mind, in your memories. Believe they hear you.

Keep moving forward, yet never get over it. Let your heart break, even as you let your heart mend. Find something that speaks to your soul. Go to nature. Go to where it's quiet. Go to holy places. Seek out the divine and seek out the human. Seek out whatever calls to your heart and fills you with meaning and purpose in this life. Realize the more purpose you have, the more you honor those who've passed through your living.

Live your life in such a way as to become a prayer of thanks for the sacred gifts that are these days, offer your tears as sanctification for all that has gone before you. Make peace with everything that didn't go the way you expected and everything that did. And if you can't make peace, then make peace with the part of yourself who can't make peace, accepting that some things in this life simply feel incomprehensible and unacceptable.

Do your best to be kind to yourself whatever your process may be. Remember you are already honoring them through the living, and breathing, and heart-beating, and feeling, and caring you have brought to this earth. This isn't about judging whether your process is right or wrong or normal—this is about doing the best you can. Just know you are a human being who has taken a rite of passage you never wanted to take. You are brave, and courageous, and full of heart and spirit for all the things you feel.

Honor you and honor them. Piece all the ways you care, and grieve, and cry, and mourn, and joy around you like a patchwork quilt, which you have stitched together with your love and depth and humanity. Wrap it around you: your super hero's cape of love that is comprised of all that you were, with all that you will be. And know each time you don that cloak, each time you look to the stars and feel the ache in your chest, each time you notice the missing and yearning and happiness and lack:

That yes, this life—*their bright light*—did indeed matter.

109

REACH THROUGH

I wonder at times what it is to be my parents.

They are in the autumn of their life, and they have lived the fear that every parent most fears: the loss of a child. I've grieved with them these past 9 months. Watched where they have tried to move through it and keep moving forward. Watched where they have splintered and cracked. Watched where they have tried to find resilience and reform. Tried as a daughter to simply be present, to make space for all of it, and offer love where I can.

This life will break your heart upside down and inside out, without any rhyme or reason; I've learned you can still keep loving anyway. I think often how Life got the seasons all wrong. Brent and I were supposed to bury Mom and Dad. Not the other way around.

Sometimes Life will do that: get it all wrong. Get the seasons all mixed up and then have the audacity to ask us to keep going and keep making new seasons. We move through and forward as best as we can, but sometimes, like the golden teardrops falling off the tree outside the window, you just have to release and make space for the starkness of grief.

Tonight I grieve for my parents. I grieve for the world and the terrible pains it holds. I grieve for a friend whose father is dying as I write these words, who is about to take her own terrible passage of losing and loving and everything that falls in between. I grieve for my brother, there is so much he never got to do, to be. And I grieve for all of those who've passed too soon, as I think about the fact that he got 39 years when there are some who get far less.

I grieve for you. For me.

If you are reading these words then you have known loss in some shape or form. Maybe your story is vastly different. Maybe it's oddly similar. Comparison doesn't really matter, for our losses—those chunks that were ripped from our hearts—are incomparable. No two will be alike, no love or grief will ever be the same.

But even so, as I sit here writing, I'm thinking about those who may read this. I'm thinking about the places you may ache, and if words can be medicine, I'm putting the intent of love and healing into mine and offering it to you in these letters. Letting my heart split and spill for the courage we all show and the fierce tenderness it takes to try for love in this space.

My parents split my heart some days; it shouldn't be like this, yet this is what it is. The longer I love and go, the more I know—you can learn to stay open anyway, smile over the spills, keep on going. Keep on loving. Keep on grieving. Keep on doing your best to stand straight, to rise up and answer the most important question that is your Life.

Sometimes I think I'm getting that question right.

Sometimes I don't even know what the question is.

Sometimes I'm just a kid who misses her brother and still can't believe he's gone.

Sometimes he comes and tells me that it was simply his time, that his work here was done and that I'm still here, because I have work left to do.

Sometimes I don't know what to think.

And sometimes he feels so close I lift my hand towards the sky, as if we are all in a giant bubble and the other side is right *there*—just a breath away—and he is lifting his hand and reaching back. If I press hard enough, I can almost reach through.

We are asked to accept some things that feel pretty unacceptable in this life. Things that are not fair, things that don't make sense, things that can't be taken back or changed. The kind of things that forever alter and reweave the fabric of who we are.

We can't do the work of grief for one another or take on each other's lessons when we have our own to learn. But we can support one another as a collective. We can make space for all of our aches and for all of the places we are finding healing. We can let our hearts split and spill and mend and repair and fill back up, and we can continue to try with ferocity and tenderness to reach for love.

Losing Brent taught me to love even harder. It's like love became my super power that got me through that dreadful time, and every time I chose to open my heart and keep believing in the goodness of life—kept choosing love—my heart got a little bit bigger, a little bit deeper, a little bit more unconditional in nature.

I don't know what it is to be my parents; I know what it is to be a daughter; I know what it is to be a sister. And in the end, that's the best that any one of us can offer: our own experiences, our own stories, our own understandings, our own wisdom. The courage to ache where we ache and make space for each other's aches.

My family is still living this story as we go. We all honor him in our own ways. Dad turns on the Patriots, makes an extra bowl of chowder for Brent, lays out his Gronkowski jersey and hopes he's out there somewhere, watching and cheering along. Mom still talks to him every day—she doesn't want him to think we've forgotten him—and posts pictures on his Facebook wall of football quotes and family photos to remind:

He was *Here*. His life meant *Something*.

As for me, I hear him in the wind. Know him when the water rushes by making everything clean and clear and new again. See him in the sky when the clouds part and the sun streams down and you can't help but know that we come from Love, were always Love, and in the end, will go back to Love. Feel him on the other side of the bubble lifting his hand, pressing, pressing, pressing…

The veil is but a wisp of illusion.

One of these days I will find a way to reach through.

110

In the end,
all that matters
is the love we have inside
and how we choose
to live it.

111

INFINITE

There will always be room for more love in our lives.

I moved through the worst season of my life in a thick gauze; feeling like the old shell of who I was had been blasted away the day the bomb dropped that Brent was gone. I was obliterated. From that moment on, I involuntarily wrapped a sheathe of grief around myself, as I went through the motions of living and, somewhere underneath that sheathe, let my skin form anew.

I was incredibly raw and achingly vulnerable and only felt half there much of the time, but even though I seemed like a shadow of self, I was still *there*. Reforming, remending, rebirthing myself into some sort of new creature who was going to emerge from this passage of grief looking different than she had before.

As time went on, I realized that every best lesson my brother taught me was one about love, which is funny if you knew him, because sometimes, he could be a hard person to love.

But none of that matters when all is said and done, because not only did that bomb burn away the old skin of who I was, it burned away all that didn't matter any more. All our imperfections and the times we didn't get it right and our ups and downs—all of those things ceased to exist, and all I was left with was this profound sense of love that I was lucky enough to have a brother in the first place, privileged enough to journey with his soul for as long and as far as I did, blessed to have known what it was to be the other half of the Dynamic Kapansky Sibling Duo.

Realize the essence of love, and you become so overwhelmed with gratitude that you can't help but go on loving, can't help but make room for more love in your life.

Nothing will ever, ever replace my brother. I will spend the rest of my life missing him, and there will always be a hole in his shape left in the heart of my family. But I can take the knowledge his death taught me—that when everything else is stripped away, all that is left is Love—and I can let it beat into my bones and work its way into my DNA and let each thrum of my heart live the truth of that knowledge.

I can write these words and hope the love they hold spreads just a little bit further. I can practice compassion, the gateway to love, doggedly. I can revel in what it is to be human and roll in what it is to be in the possibility of *right now*. I can embrace my relationships for all I'm worth, love myself for all I'm worth, take this new skin of self and live to the best of my ability.

Nobody's grief passage will ever look the same, but for me, after the jagged mountains, the desolate wasteland, the relentless desert, that deep long ocean of sadness, I washed up onto new shore.

Gradually got my feet underneath me and remembered I knew how to walk. Stepped out onto a landscape of gentle, shimmering pink where billions upon billions of stars light the way in the night, and the sun brings warmth and renewal each day. And I could see the invisible, gossamer strands of love running through it all. Wrapping everything together, connecting us in our shared humanity, holding us in place in the grace of this space.

Love has no walls here.

The possibilities are infinite.

In loving memory of
Brother Skywalker

Brent Michael Kapansky

6/13/1976 – 1/18/2016

Auf Wiedersehen and Thank You

How do you end a story whose truths you are still living?

You don't. You simply say farewell for now and then go about the story of living new truths.

Today marks the 10 month anniversary of losing my brother. So little time, yet so much time, captured between these pages. As I went about the business of writing and assembling *Lamentations of The Sea*, I often wondered at the wisdom of writing a book on loss, while one is still processing their own. So much of it is still so close to my heart and still so close to where I now find myself on my timeline.

This wasn't a reflection or remembrance that took on the kind of soft, nostalgic tints we find in old photographs; it was a story that was written as I went, a graphic novel that bleeds out all over the pages even as it heals itself back up by the very things which causes it to bleed: love. Love is the essence of this story, and it is the question and the answer.

Some of the material took a bit of emotional courage to dive back into, and there were moments where I wondered if I was ready to share these moments. Strong enough to share these deepest recesses of grief? Open enough to bare my heart and gain someone entrance to such tragic, personal material? Healed up enough to share what is most wounded and beautiful and aching and true inside of myself?

And then I realized none of those questions really matter, because at the end of the day all any of us can do is listen to ourselves and proceed with life as best we know how. Each of us has that still small voice inside of ourselves, our own requirements of soul that must be met. And sometimes, that voice can be rather insistent and pressing, challenging us to do brave things, whether or not we feel ready.

And whenever I had doubts about this work, I would sit in quiet and listen to my own requirements of soul, find that voice inside of myself. My heart has a way of cutting through all the mental chatter and making clear what is evident to her. And over and over again she kept saying:

Write the book. Write the book. Write the book.

I wrote the book.

And I hope these words offered some measure of solace, healing and restoration to anyone who walked through these pages and stories with me.

There are a few sources of inspiration that have woven themselves into these words. *The Love Inside* was inspired by a line from the movie *Ghost* where Sam says to Molly, "It's amazing Molly. The love inside, you take it with you." The last line in *Oh Brother Where Art Though* was inspired by the final line in the movie *Gladiator*, "Now we are free. I will see you again, but not yet. Not yet." Last, the line "open at the close" was inspired by J.K. Rowling's *Harry Potter and the Deathly Hallows*, when Dumbledore gifts the golden snitch to Harry with the engraved words, "I open at the close." These words not only provided inspiration for my brother's eulogy, as referenced in *The Longest Walk*, but also became the theme and inspiration for the poem *Open at the Close*.

Reach and *Bounce* were originally published through *Rebelle Society*. *Seas of Infinity* was originally published through *When Women Waken, Water Issue* (edited by Anora McGaha), and *Relentless Gratitude* was originally published through *Women's Spiritual Poetry Project*, (founded by Catherine Schweig). I gratefully acknowledge and thank all for their support of my work.

In no particular order and with all particular thanks: Linda Webber, Amy Barker Smith, Gloria Petruzzelli, Cynthia Bolivar, Hillary Walker, April M. Lee, and Leslie Cornick—THANK YOU!—you wonderful, wonderful women. I appreciate the time you took to review this manuscript and all your words of support. I feel so grateful and fortunate to be surrounded by such a beautiful group of women who bring so many talents to this world, professionally and personally. Thank you from my heart.

Alice Maldonado Gallardo, thank you for saying yes to my work, again! Golden Dragonfly Press has given me a tremendous forum in which to publish, and it is a joy and pleasure to work with you and the creativity, quality, and talent you bring to the process. It is so good to know you Alice.